HOWE·LIBRARY

HANOVER
NEW HAMPSHIRE

D1457206

The Mystery of
Mary Rogers

ISBN 1-56163-274-0 hc
ISBN 1-56163-288-0 pb
Library of Congress Catalog Card Number 00-111789
©2001 Rick Geary
Printed in China

5   4   3   2

Comicslit is an imprint and
trademark of

NANTIER · BEALL · MINOUSTCHINE
Publishing inc.
new york

The Mystery of Mary Rogers

A CHRONICLE OF
THE DISAPPEARANCE AND MURDER OF
"THE BEAUTIFUL SEGAR GIRL"
IN JULY, 1841 —

A CRIME WHICH
WAS NEVER SOLVED —

BROADWAY

THE NEW JERSEY
SHORE

AND WHICH INSPIRED THE
SENSATIONAL TALE BY
EDGAR A. POE

COMPILED AND ILLUSTRATED BY
RICK GEARY

Also available by Geary:
A Treasury of Victorian Murder:
Jack The Ripper, hc: $15.95
The Borden Tragedy, pb: $8.95
The Fatal Bullet, pb: $8.95

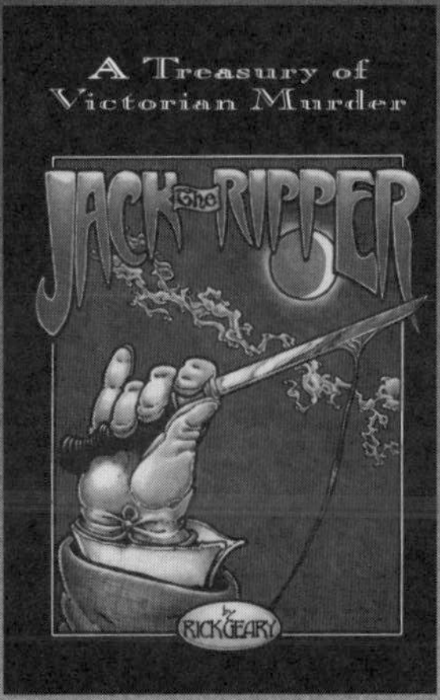
A Treasury of Victorian Murder
Jack the Ripper
by Rick Geary

We have over 150 titles, write
for our color catalog:
NBM
555 8th Ave. Suite 1202,
New York, NY 10018
see our website at
http://www.nbmpublishing.com

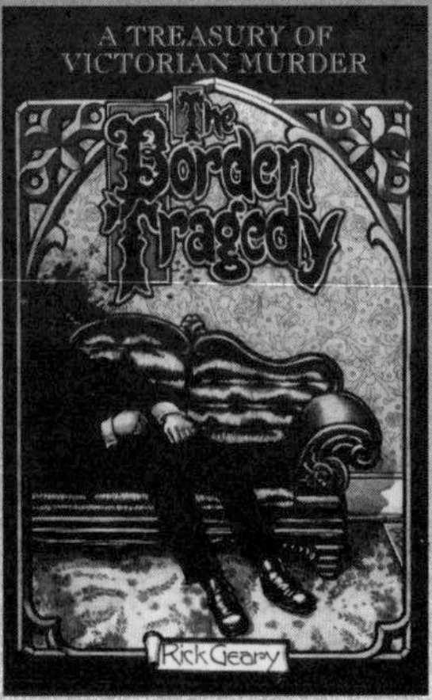
A TREASURY OF VICTORIAN MURDER
The Borden Tragedy
Rick Geary

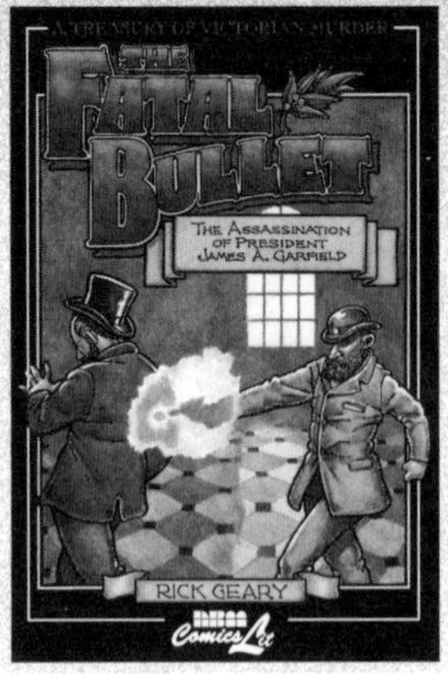
A TREASURY OF VICTORIAN MURDER
THE FATAL BULLET
THE ASSASSINATION OF PRESIDENT JAMES A. GARFIELD
RICK GEARY
ComicsLit

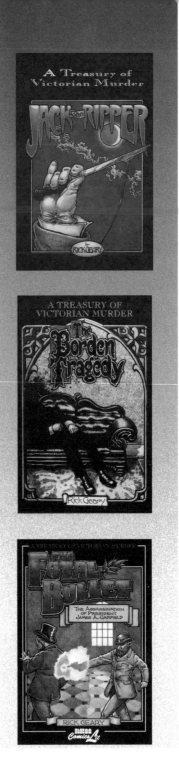

BIBLIOGRAPHY

Burroughs, Edwin G. and Mike Wallace, *Gotham, A History of New York City to 1898*. (New York, Oxford University Press, 1999)

Byrnes, Thomas, *1886 Professional Criminals of America*. (New York, Chelsea House, 1969)

Cohen, Paul E. and Robert T. Augustyn, *Manhattan in Maps 1527-1995*. (New York, Rizzoli, 1997)

Homberger, Eric, *The Historical Atlas of New York City*. (New York, Henry Holt and Co., 1994)

Paul, Raymond, *Who Murdered Mary Rogers?* (Englewood Cliffs, NJ, Prentice Hall, 1971)

Poe, Edgar Allan, "The Mystery of Marie Roget," reprinted in *Great Tales and Poems of Edgar Allan Poe*. (New York, Pocket Books, 1951)

Silverman, Kenneth, *Edgar Allan Poe, Mournul and Never-Ending Remembrance*. (New York, Harper Collins, 1992)

Srebnick, Amy Gilman, *The Mysterious Death of Mary Rogers*. (New York, Oxford University Press, 1995)

Wallace, Irving, "The Real Marie Roget," reprinted in *The Mammoth Book of Unsolved Crimes*. (New York, Carroll & Graf Publishers, Inc., 1999)

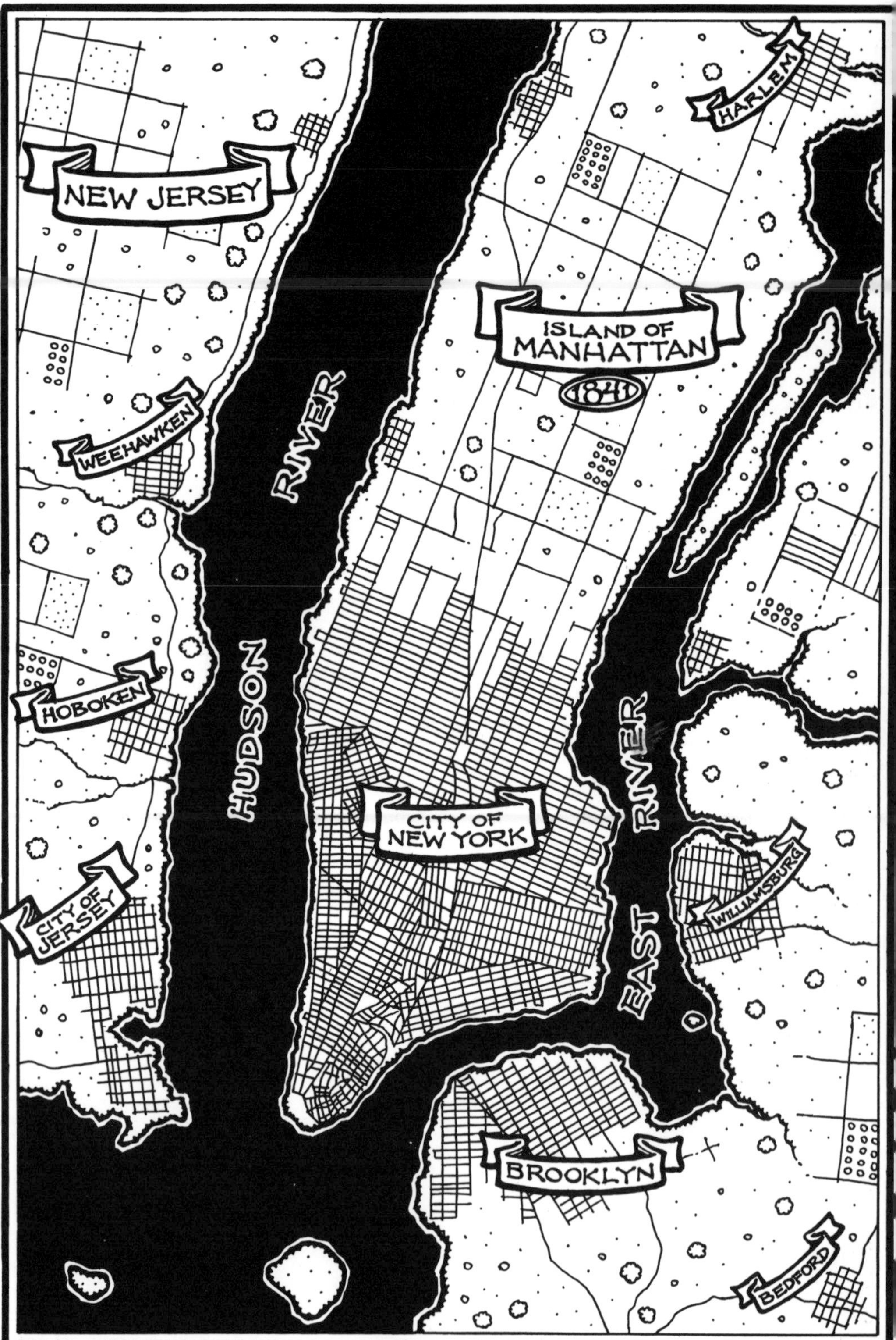
NEW JERSEY
HARLEM
ISLAND OF MANHATTAN
1841
WEEHAWKEN
HUDSON RIVER
HOBOKEN
CITY OF NEW YORK
EAST RIVER
CITY OF JERSEY
WILLIAMSBURG
BROOKLYN
BEDFORD

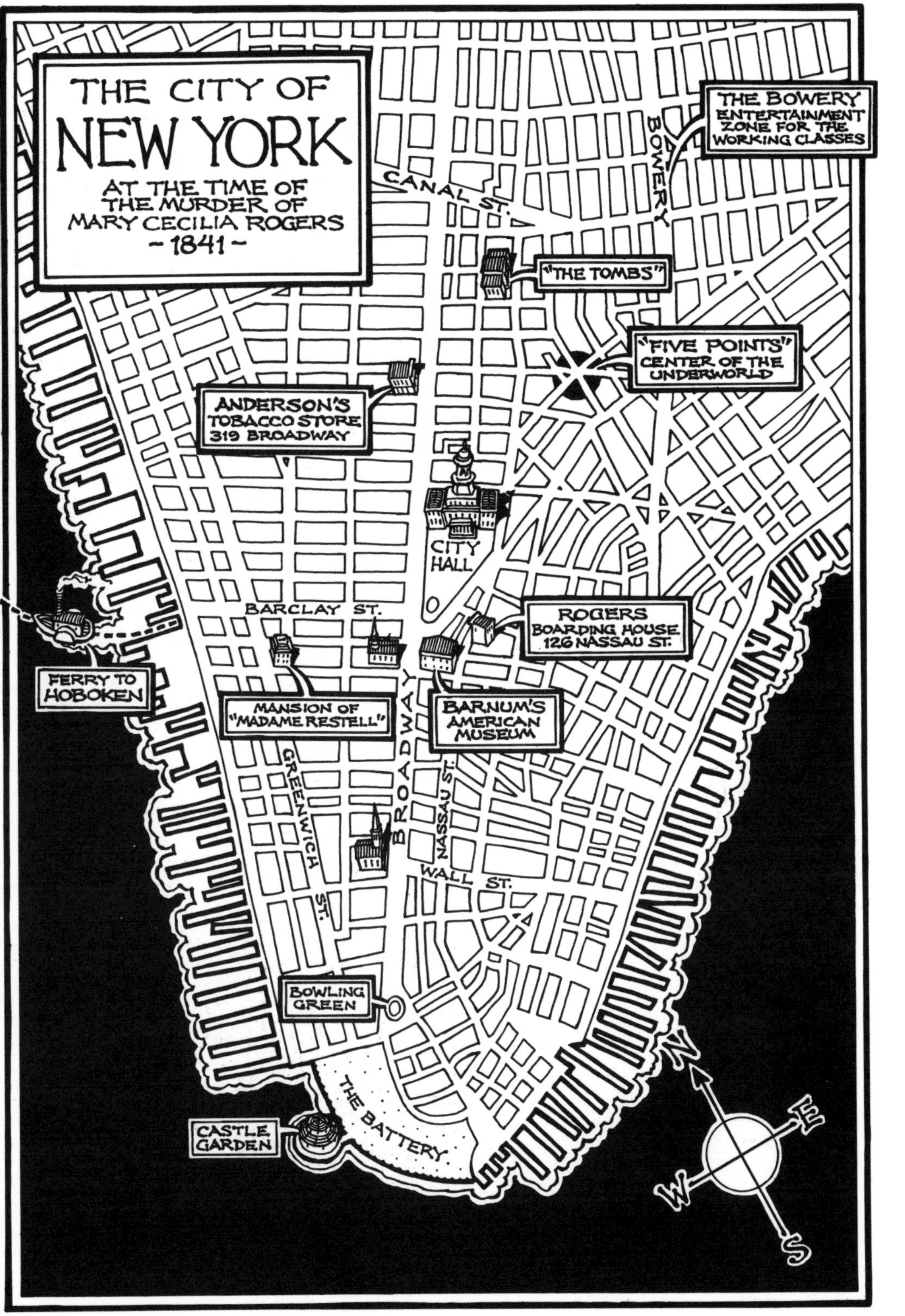
THE CITY OF
NEW YORK
AT THE TIME OF
THE MURDER OF
MARY CECILIA ROGERS
-1841-
THE BOWERY
ENTERTAINMENT ZONE FOR THE WORKING CLASSES
BOWERY
CANAL ST.
"THE TOMBS"
"FIVE POINTS"
CENTER OF THE UNDERWORLD
ANDERSON'S
TOBACCO STORE
319 BROADWAY
CITY HALL
BARCLAY ST.
ROGERS
BOARDING HOUSE
126 NASSAU ST.
FERRY TO HOBOKEN
MANSION OF "MADAME RESTELL"
BARNUM'S
AMERICAN
MUSEUM
GREENWICH ST.
BROADWAY
NASSAU ST.
WALL ST.
BOWLING GREEN
THE BATTERY
CASTLE GARDEN
N
E
W
S

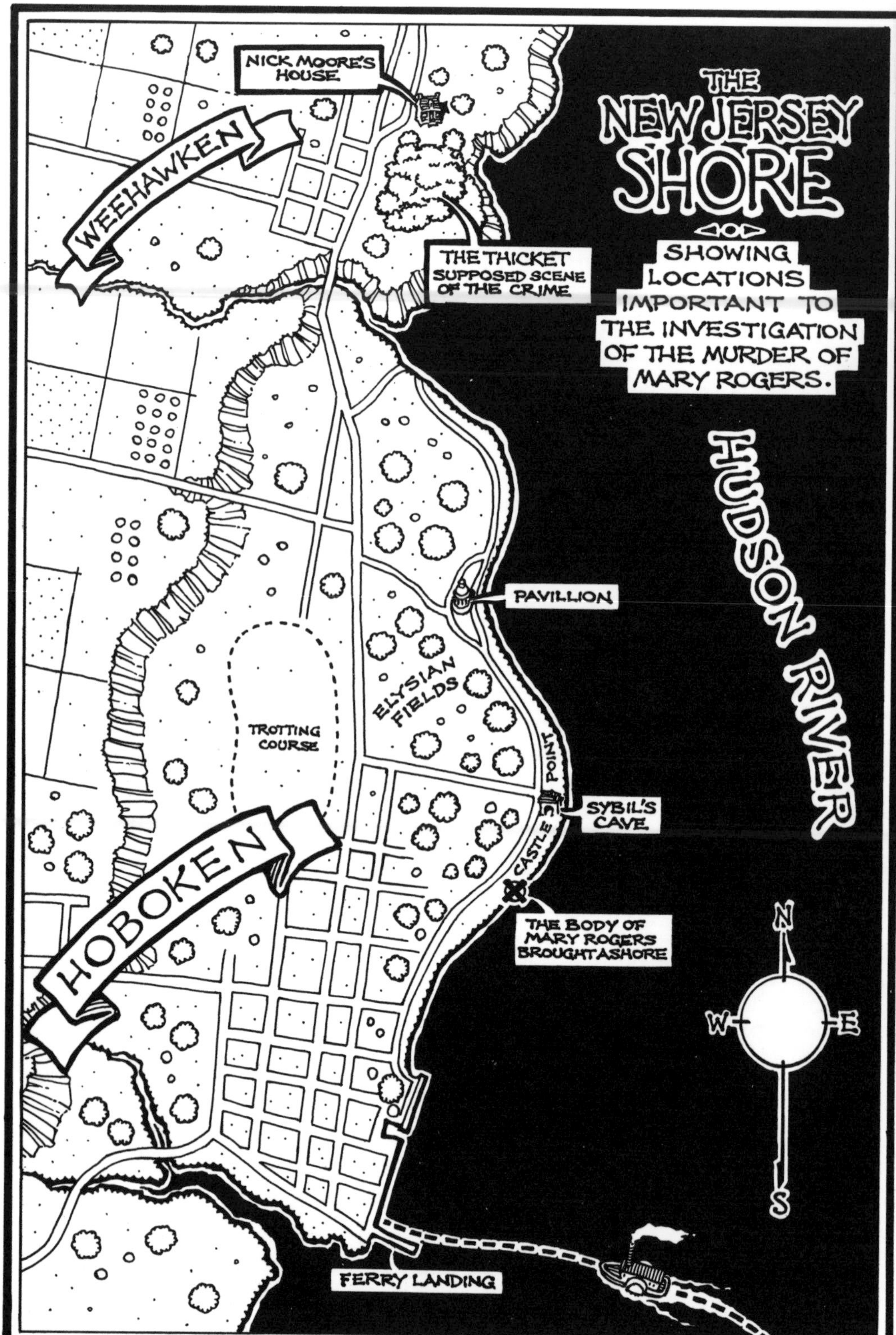
THE NEW JERSEY SHORE
SHOWING LOCATIONS IMPORTANT TO THE INVESTIGATION OF THE MURDER OF MARY ROGERS.
NICK MOORE'S HOUSE
WEEHAWKEN
THE THICKET SUPPOSED SCENE OF THE CRIME
HUDSON RIVER
PAVILLION
ELYSIAN FIELDS
TROTTING COURSE
CASTLE POINT
SYBIL'S CAVE
THE BODY OF MARY ROGERS BROUGHT ASHORE
HOBOKEN
FERRY LANDING
N
W
E
S

PART I.

A BODY IN
THE RIVER

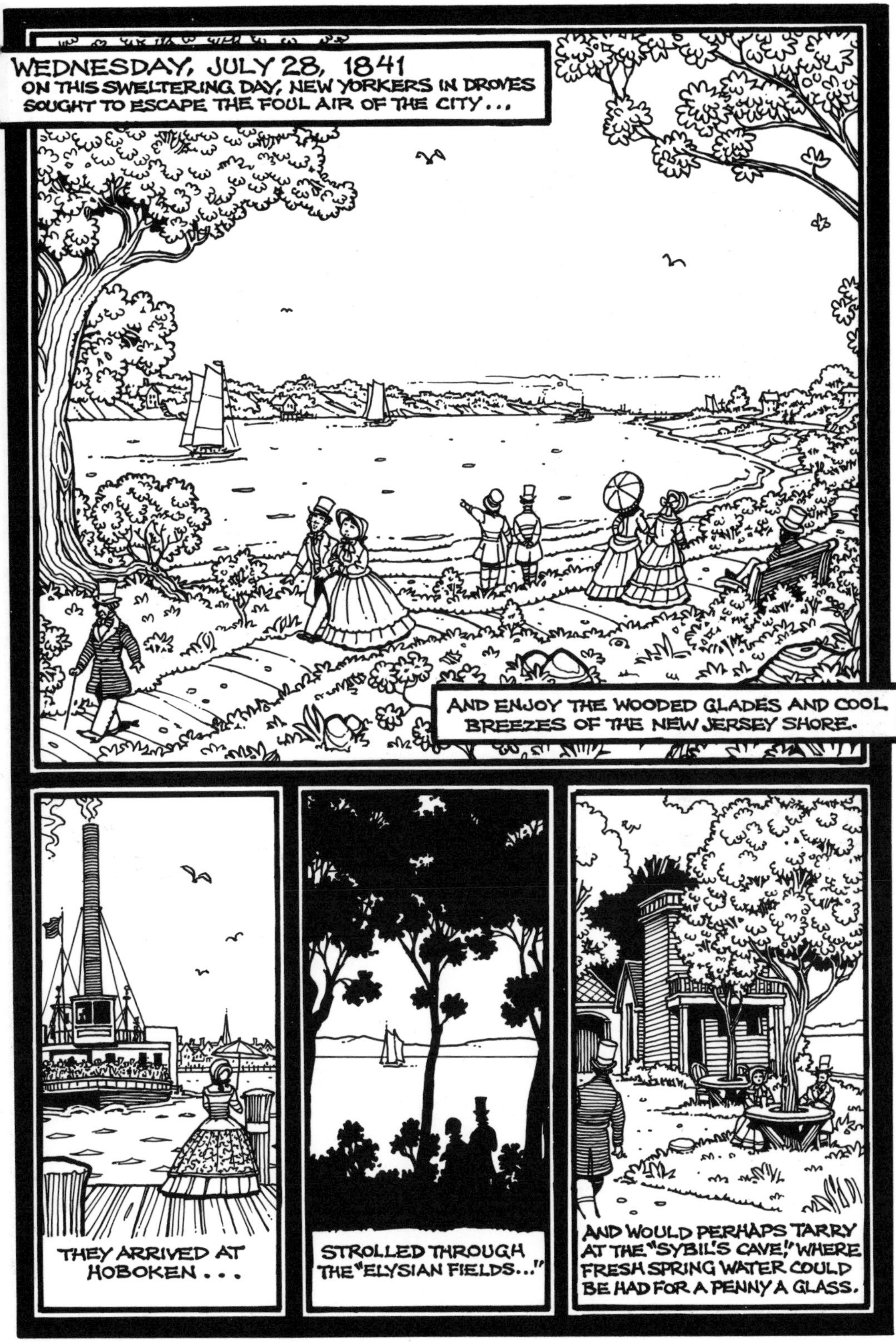
WEDNESDAY, JULY 28, 1841
ON THIS SWELTERING DAY, NEW YORKERS IN DROVES SOUGHT TO ESCAPE THE FOUL AIR OF THE CITY...
AND ENJOY THE WOODED GLADES AND COOL BREEZES OF THE NEW JERSEY SHORE.
THEY ARRIVED AT HOBOKEN...
STROLLED THROUGH THE "ELYSIAN FIELDS..."
AND WOULD PERHAPS TARRY AT THE "SYBIL'S CAVE," WHERE FRESH SPRING WATER COULD BE HAD FOR A PENNY A GLASS.

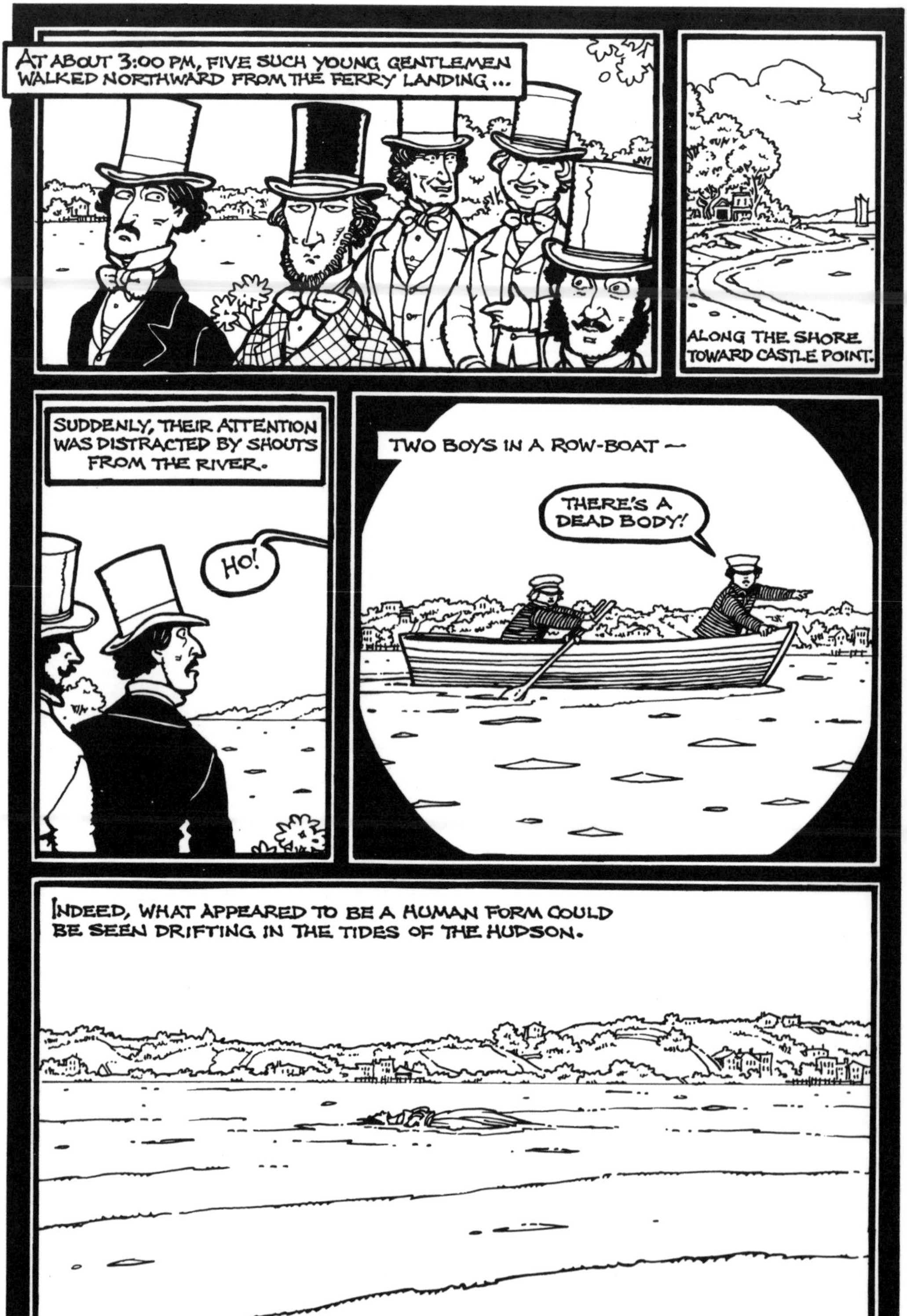
AT ABOUT 3:00 PM, FIVE SUCH YOUNG GENTLEMEN WALKED NORTHWARD FROM THE FERRY LANDING...
ALONG THE SHORE TOWARD CASTLE POINT.
SUDDENLY, THEIR ATTENTION WAS DISTRACTED BY SHOUTS FROM THE RIVER.
HO!
TWO BOYS IN A ROW-BOAT —
THERE'S A DEAD BODY!
INDEED, WHAT APPEARED TO BE A HUMAN FORM COULD BE SEEN DRIFTING IN THE TIDES OF THE HUDSON.

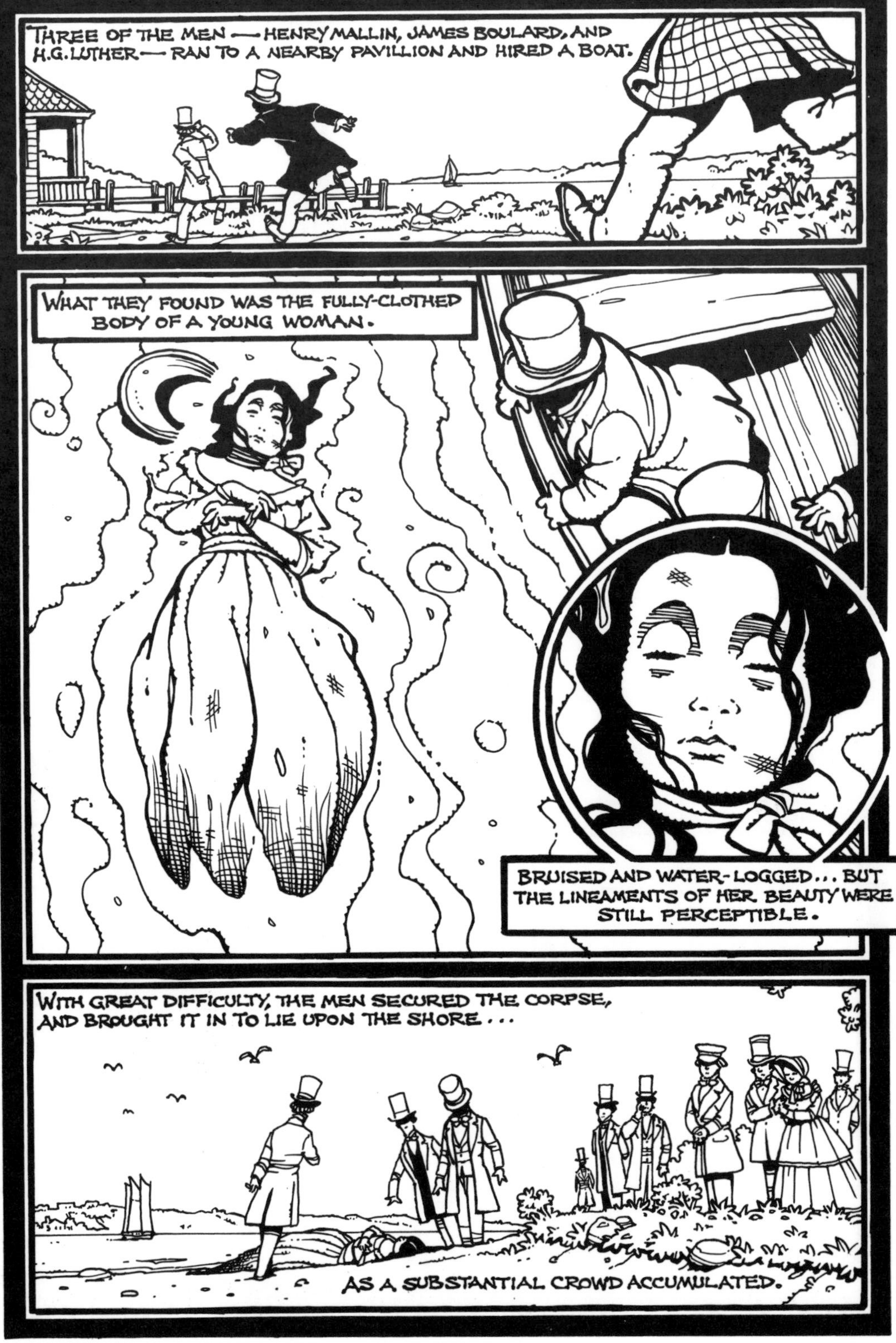
THREE OF THE MEN — HENRY MALLIN, JAMES BOULARD, AND H.G. LUTHER — RAN TO A NEARBY PAVILLION AND HIRED A BOAT.
WHAT THEY FOUND WAS THE FULLY-CLOTHED BODY OF A YOUNG WOMAN.
BRUISED AND WATER-LOGGED... BUT THE LINEAMENTS OF HER BEAUTY WERE STILL PERCEPTIBLE.
WITH GREAT DIFFICULTY, THE MEN SECURED THE CORPSE, AND BROUGHT IT IN TO LIE UPON THE SHORE...
AS A SUBSTANTIAL CROWD ACCUMULATED.

BEFORE LONG, TWO YOUNG MEN EMERGED FROM THE CROWD TO EXAMINE THE REMAINS CLOSELY.

DEAR GOD...

THEY KNEW THE UNFORTUNATE YOUNG LADY.

THIS IS MARY ROGERS!

OH GOD — THE NEWS MAY KILL HER MOTHER!

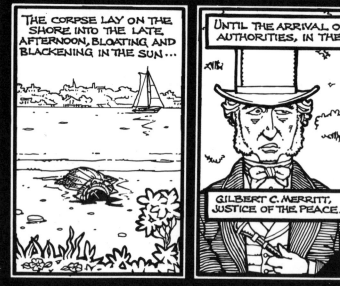

THE CORPSE LAY ON THE SHORE INTO THE LATE AFTERNOON, BLOATING AND BLACKENING IN THE SUN...

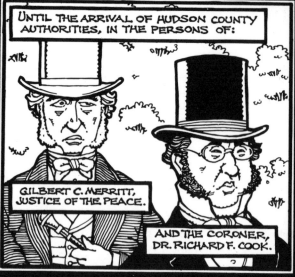

UNTIL THE ARRIVAL OF HUDSON COUNTY AUTHORITIES, IN THE PERSONS OF:

GILBERT C. MERRITT, JUSTICE OF THE PEACE.

AND THE CORONER, DR. RICHARD F. COOK.

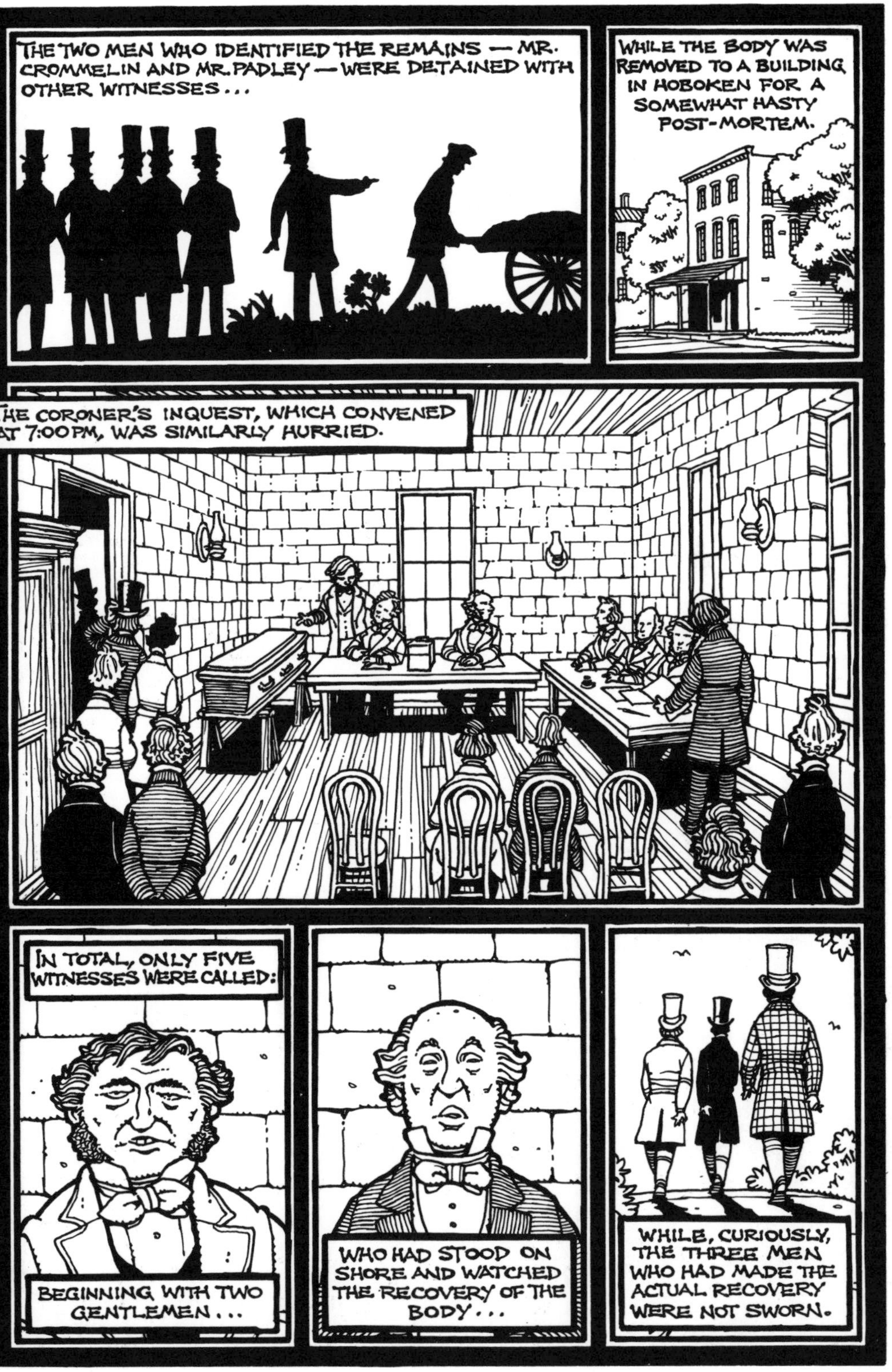
THE TWO MEN WHO IDENTIFIED THE REMAINS — MR. CROMMELIN AND MR. PADLEY — WERE DETAINED WITH OTHER WITNESSES...
WHILE THE BODY WAS REMOVED TO A BUILDING IN HOBOKEN FOR A SOMEWHAT HASTY POST-MORTEM.
THE CORONER'S INQUEST, WHICH CONVENED AT 7:00 PM, WAS SIMILARLY HURRIED.
IN TOTAL, ONLY FIVE WITNESSES WERE CALLED:
BEGINNING WITH TWO GENTLEMEN...
WHO HAD STOOD ON SHORE AND WATCHED THE RECOVERY OF THE BODY...
WHILE, CURIOUSLY, THE THREE MEN WHO HAD MADE THE ACTUAL RECOVERY WERE NOT SWORN.

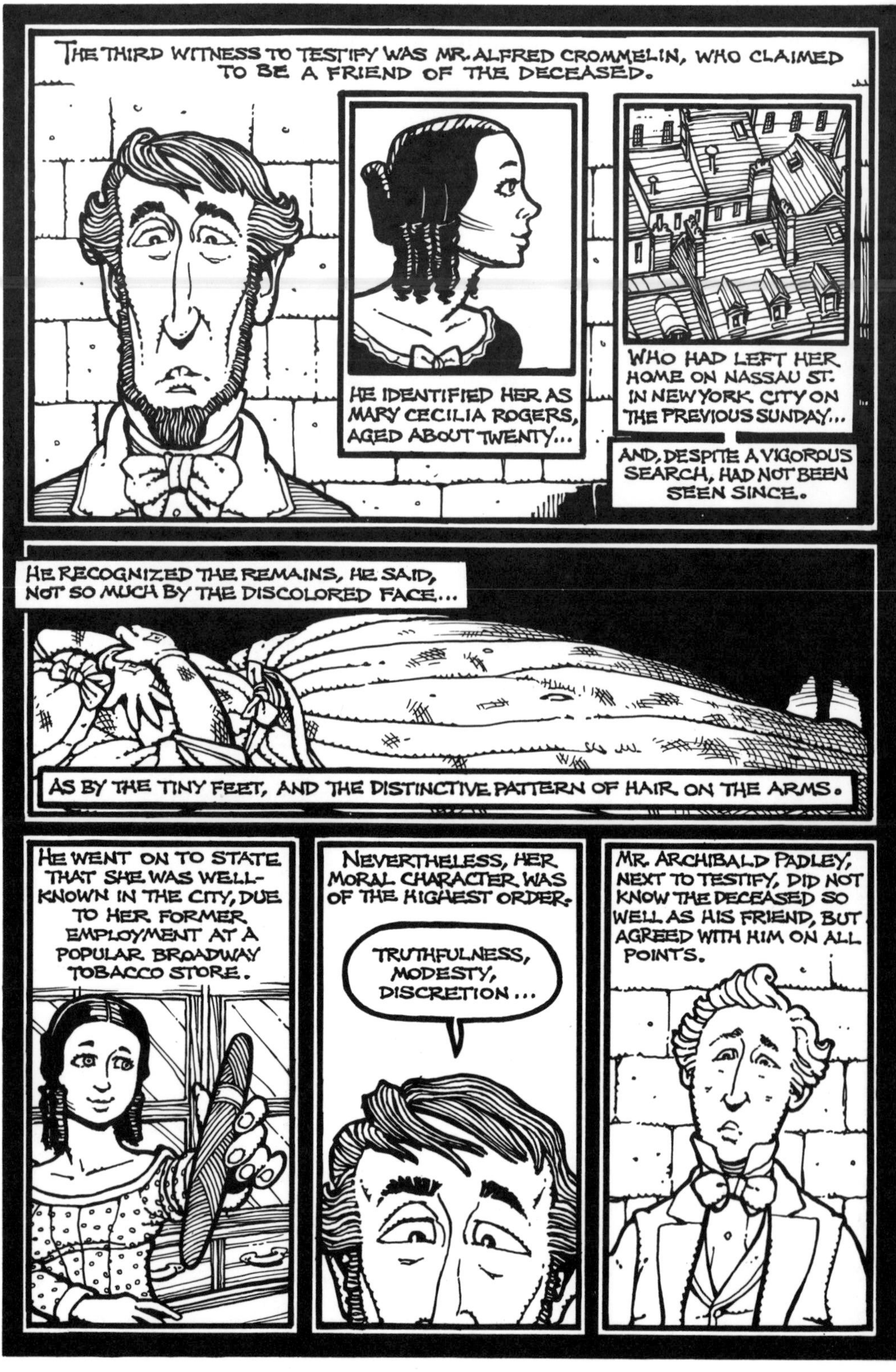
THE THIRD WITNESS TO TESTIFY WAS MR. ALFRED CROMMELIN, WHO CLAIMED TO BE A FRIEND OF THE DECEASED.
HE IDENTIFIED HER AS MARY CECILIA ROGERS, AGED ABOUT TWENTY...
WHO HAD LEFT HER HOME ON NASSAU ST. IN NEW YORK CITY ON THE PREVIOUS SUNDAY...
AND, DESPITE A VIGOROUS SEARCH, HAD NOT BEEN SEEN SINCE.
HE RECOGNIZED THE REMAINS, HE SAID, NOT SO MUCH BY THE DISCOLORED FACE...
AS BY THE TINY FEET, AND THE DISTINCTIVE PATTERN OF HAIR ON THE ARMS.
HE WENT ON TO STATE THAT SHE WAS WELL-KNOWN IN THE CITY, DUE TO HER FORMER EMPLOYMENT AT A POPULAR BROADWAY TOBACCO STORE.
NEVERTHELESS, HER MORAL CHARACTER WAS OF THE HIGHEST ORDER.
TRUTHFULNESS, MODESTY, DISCRETION...
MR. ARCHIBALD PADLEY, NEXT TO TESTIFY, DID NOT KNOW THE DECEASED SO WELL AS HIS FRIEND, BUT AGREED WITH HIM ON ALL POINTS.

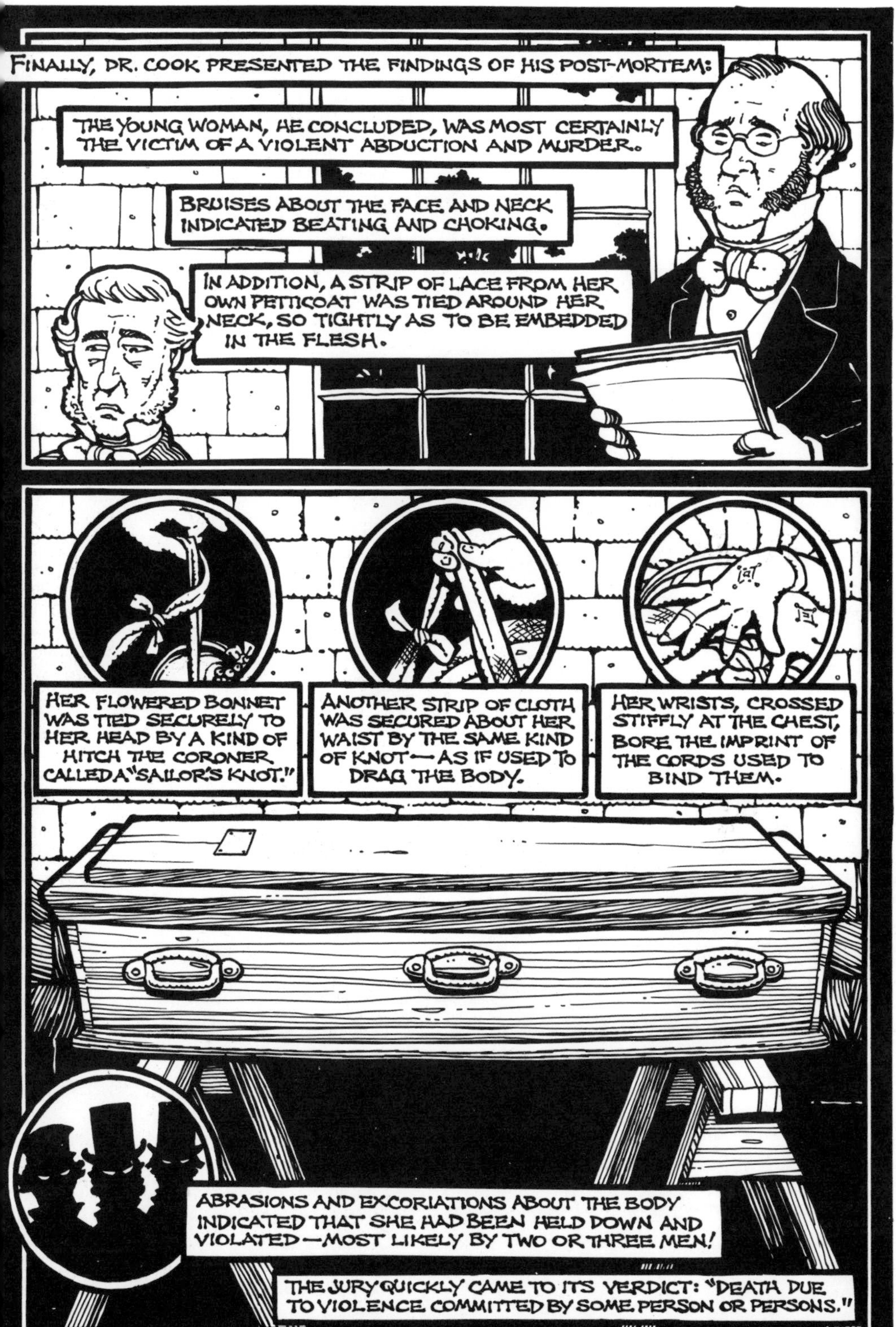
FINALLY, DR. COOK PRESENTED THE FINDINGS OF HIS POST-MORTEM:
THE YOUNG WOMAN, HE CONCLUDED, WAS MOST CERTAINLY THE VICTIM OF A VIOLENT ABDUCTION AND MURDER.
BRUISES ABOUT THE FACE AND NECK INDICATED BEATING AND CHOKING.
IN ADDITION, A STRIP OF LACE FROM HER OWN PETTICOAT WAS TIED AROUND HER NECK, SO TIGHTLY AS TO BE EMBEDDED IN THE FLESH.
HER FLOWERED BONNET WAS TIED SECURELY TO HER HEAD BY A KIND OF HITCH THE CORONER CALLED A "SAILOR'S KNOT."
ANOTHER STRIP OF CLOTH WAS SECURED ABOUT HER WAIST BY THE SAME KIND OF KNOT — AS IF USED TO DRAG THE BODY.
HER WRISTS, CROSSED STIFFLY AT THE CHEST, BORE THE IMPRINT OF THE CORDS USED TO BIND THEM.
ABRASIONS AND EXCORIATIONS ABOUT THE BODY INDICATED THAT SHE HAD BEEN HELD DOWN AND VIOLATED — MOST LIKELY BY TWO OR THREE MEN!
THE JURY QUICKLY CAME TO ITS VERDICT: "DEATH DUE TO VIOLENCE COMMITTED BY SOME PERSON OR PERSONS."

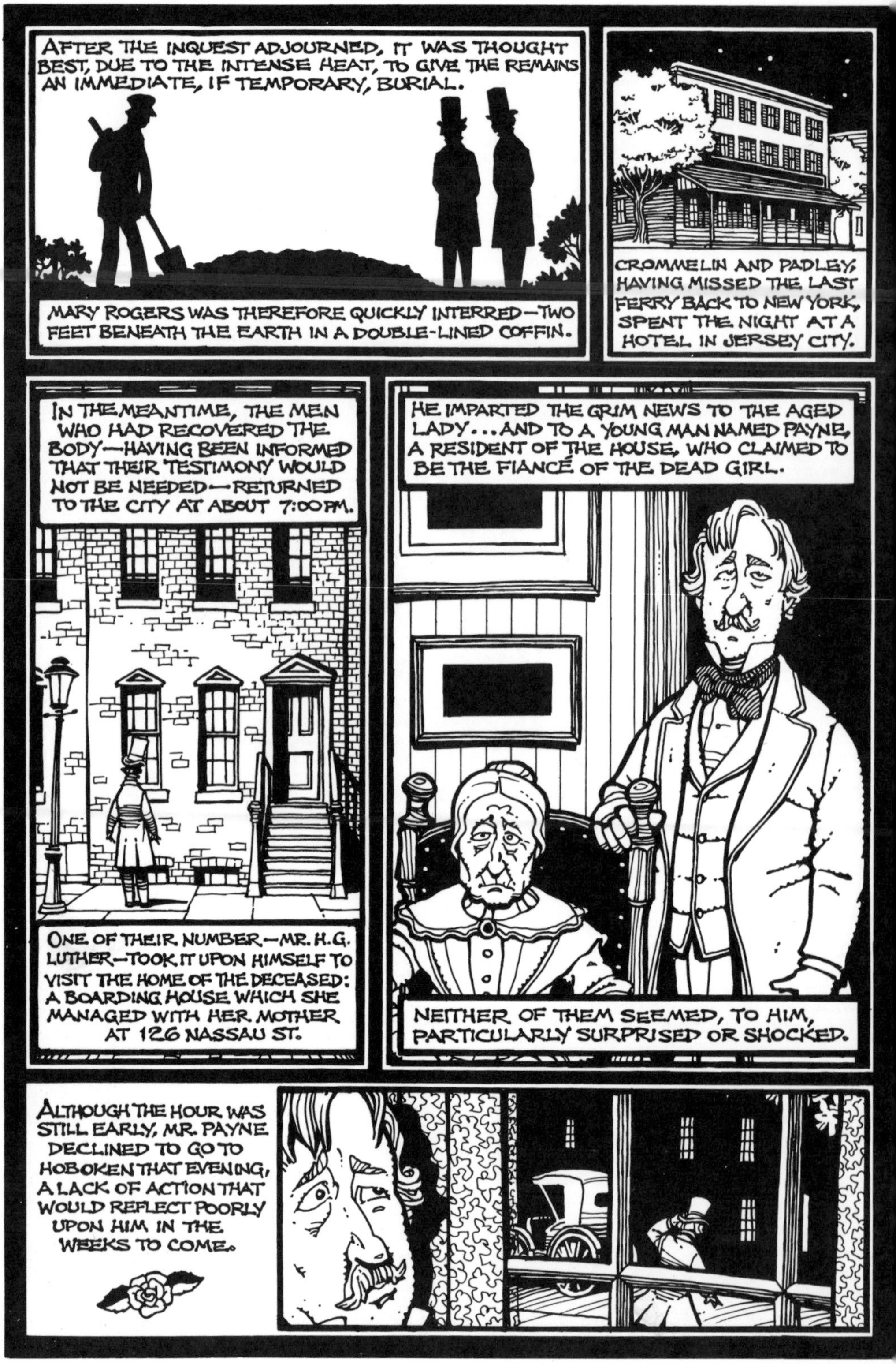

AFTER THE INQUEST ADJOURNED, IT WAS THOUGHT BEST, DUE TO THE INTENSE HEAT, TO GIVE THE REMAINS AN IMMEDIATE, IF TEMPORARY, BURIAL.
MARY ROGERS WAS THEREFORE QUICKLY INTERRED—TWO FEET BENEATH THE EARTH IN A DOUBLE-LINED COFFIN.
CROMMELIN AND PADLEY, HAVING MISSED THE LAST FERRY BACK TO NEW YORK, SPENT THE NIGHT AT A HOTEL IN JERSEY CITY.
IN THE MEANTIME, THE MEN WHO HAD RECOVERED THE BODY—HAVING BEEN INFORMED THAT THEIR TESTIMONY WOULD NOT BE NEEDED—RETURNED TO THE CITY AT ABOUT 7:00 P.M.
ONE OF THEIR NUMBER—MR. H.G. LUTHER—TOOK IT UPON HIMSELF TO VISIT THE HOME OF THE DECEASED: A BOARDING HOUSE WHICH SHE MANAGED WITH HER MOTHER AT 126 NASSAU ST.
HE IMPARTED THE GRIM NEWS TO THE AGED LADY...AND TO A YOUNG MAN NAMED PAYNE, A RESIDENT OF THE HOUSE, WHO CLAIMED TO BE THE FIANCÉ OF THE DEAD GIRL.
NEITHER OF THEM SEEMED, TO HIM, PARTICULARLY SURPRISED OR SHOCKED.
ALTHOUGH THE HOUR WAS STILL EARLY, MR. PAYNE DECLINED TO GO TO HOBOKEN THAT EVENING, A LACK OF ACTION THAT WOULD REFLECT POORLY UPON HIM IN THE WEEKS TO COME.

THURSDAY, JULY 29 —
ON THAT MORNING, CROMMELIN AND PADLEY
RETURNED TO THE CITY AND PAID A CALL
UPON THE GRIEVING MRS. ROGERS.

THEY DISPLAYED FOR HER AN ARRAY OF IDENTIFYING ITEMS GIVEN THEM BY THE CORONER...

INCLUDING EVEN A LOCK OF MARY'S HAIR—

IN THE DAYS THAT FOLLOWED, ANY KIND OF OFFICIAL INVESTIGATION WAS FRUSTRATED BY A JURISDICTIONAL DISPUTE:

THE NEW YORK AUTHORITIES DECLARED IT A NEW JERSEY CASE...

WHILE NEW JERSEY OFFICIALS FELT THAT, SINCE THE VICTIM WAS A CITY RESIDENT, THE CASE SHOULD BE NEW YORK'S. (AFTER ALL, WERE NOT THE VICTIMS OF THE CITY'S CRIMES CONSTANTLY WASHING UP ON THE SHORES OF NEW JERSEY?)

FRIDAY, JULY 30 — ON THAT MORNING, WORD WAS ABROAD OF THE MURDER OF THE "BEAUTIFUL SEGAR GIRL."

SUNDAY, AUGUST 1 — SAW THE FIRST NEWSPAPER NOTICE— IN THE SUNDAY MERCURY...

AND BY THE NEXT MORNING, THE CRIME WAS FEATURED IN EACH OF THE CITY'S NUMEROUS DAILY JOURNALS.

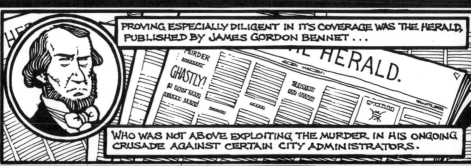

PROVING ESPECIALLY DILIGENT IN ITS COVERAGE WAS THE HERALD, PUBLISHED BY JAMES GORDON BENNET...

MURDER

GHASTLY!

THE HERALD.

WHO WAS NOT ABOVE EXPLOITING THE MURDER IN HIS ONGOING CRUSADE AGAINST CERTAIN CITY ADMINISTRATORS.

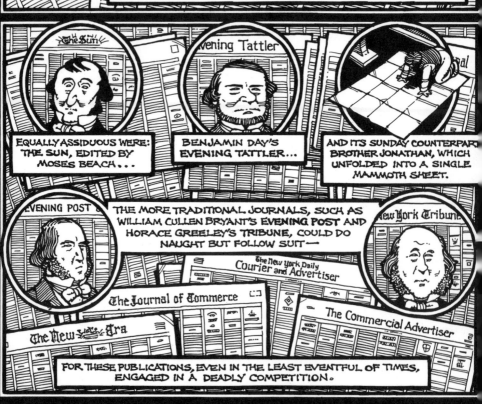

The Sun

Evening Tattler

EQUALLY ASSIDUOUS WERE: THE SUN, EDITED BY MOSES BEACH...

BENJAMIN DAY'S EVENING TATTLER...

AND ITS SUNDAY COUNTERPART BROTHER JONATHAN, WHICH UNFOLDED INTO A SINGLE MAMMOTH SHEET.

EVENING POST

THE MORE TRADITIONAL JOURNALS, SUCH AS WILLIAM CULLEN BRYANT'S EVENING POST AND HORACE GREELEY'S TRIBUNE, COULD DO NAUGHT BUT FOLLOW SUIT—

New York Tribune

The New York Daily Courier and Advertiser

The Journal of Commerce

The Commercial Advertiser

The New Era

FOR THESE PUBLICATIONS, EVEN IN THE LEAST EVENTFUL OF TIMES, ENGAGED IN A DEADLY COMPETITION.

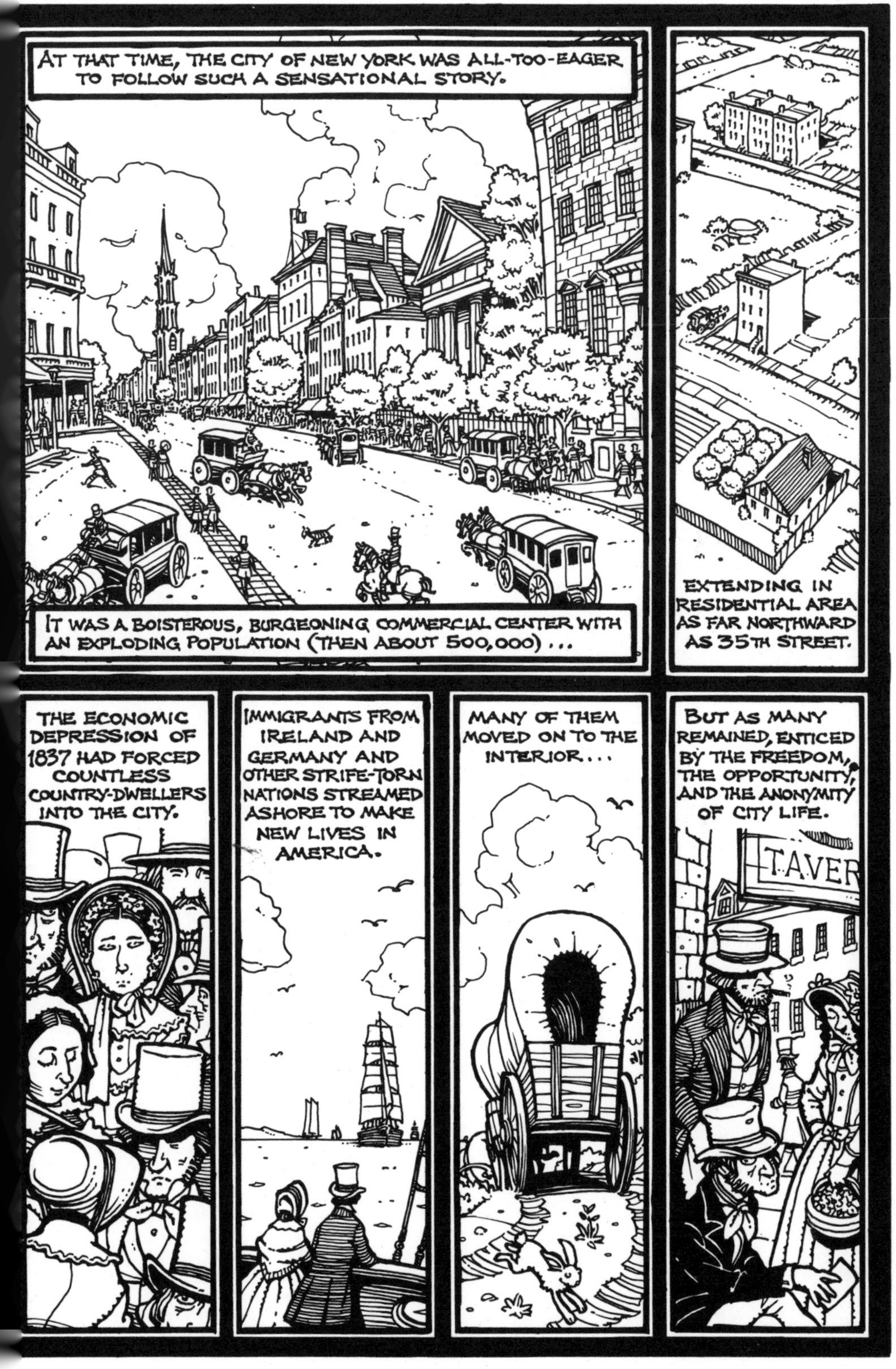

AT THAT TIME, THE CITY OF NEW YORK WAS ALL-TOO-EAGER TO FOLLOW SUCH A SENSATIONAL STORY.
IT WAS A BOISTEROUS, BURGEONING COMMERCIAL CENTER WITH AN EXPLODING POPULATION (THEN ABOUT 500,000)...
EXTENDING IN RESIDENTIAL AREA AS FAR NORTHWARD AS 35TH STREET.
THE ECONOMIC DEPRESSION OF 1837 HAD FORCED COUNTLESS COUNTRY-DWELLERS INTO THE CITY.
IMMIGRANTS FROM IRELAND AND GERMANY AND OTHER STRIFE-TORN NATIONS STREAMED ASHORE TO MAKE NEW LIVES IN AMERICA.
MANY OF THEM MOVED ON TO THE INTERIOR...
BUT AS MANY REMAINED, ENTICED BY THE FREEDOM, THE OPPORTUNITY, AND THE ANONYMITY OF CITY LIFE.
TAVER

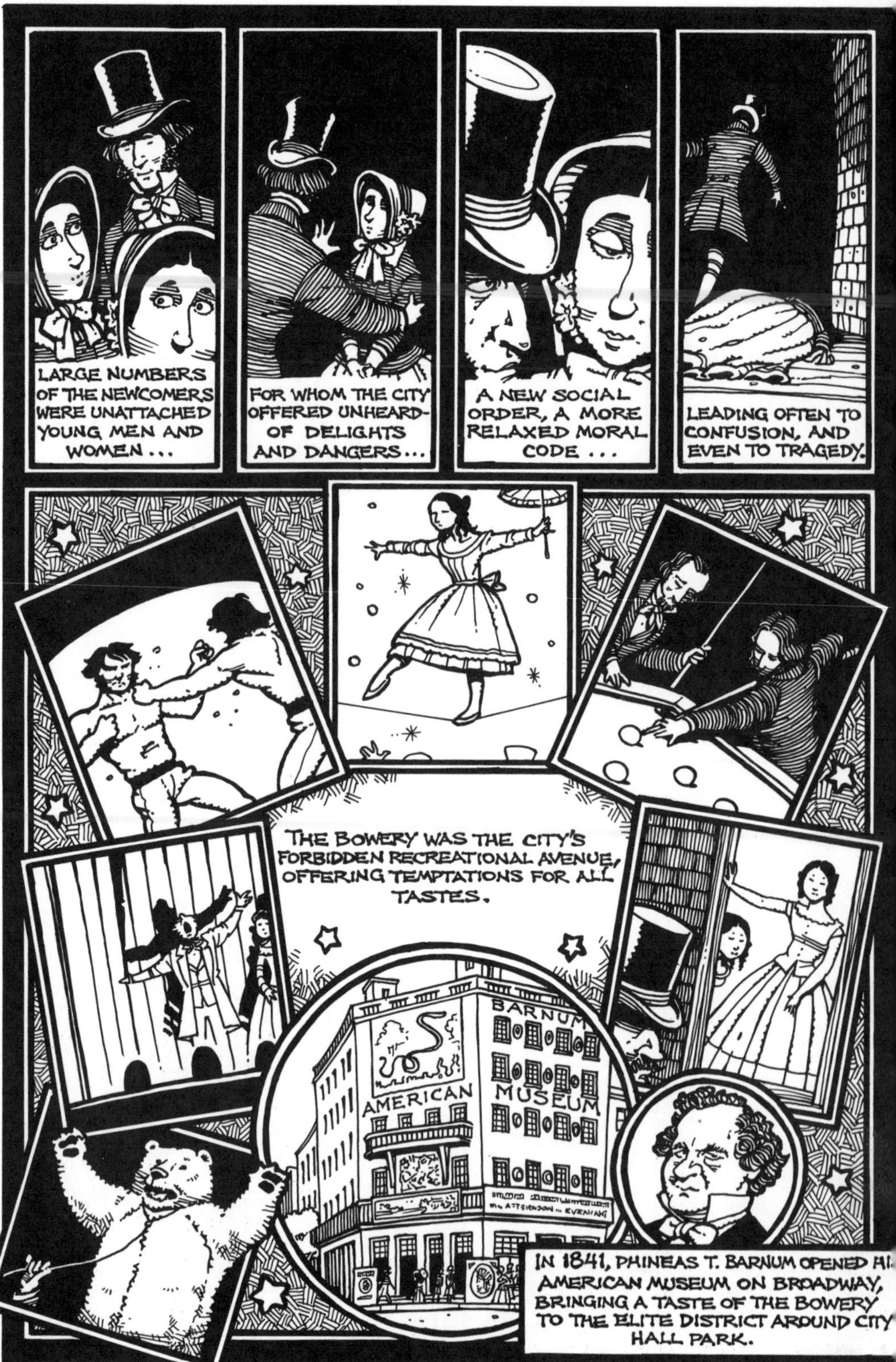
LARGE NUMBERS OF THE NEWCOMERS WERE UNATTACHED YOUNG MEN AND WOMEN . . .
FOR WHOM THE CITY OFFERED UNHEARD-OF DELIGHTS AND DANGERS . . .
A NEW SOCIAL ORDER, A MORE RELAXED MORAL CODE . . .
LEADING OFTEN TO CONFUSION, AND EVEN TO TRAGEDY.
THE BOWERY WAS THE CITY'S FORBIDDEN RECREATIONAL AVENUE, OFFERING TEMPTATIONS FOR ALL TASTES.
AMERICAN
BARNUM
MUSEUM
IN 1841, PHINEAS T. BARNUM OPENED HI AMERICAN MUSEUM ON BROADWAY, BRINGING A TASTE OF THE BOWERY TO THE ELITE DISTRICT AROUND CITY HALL PARK.

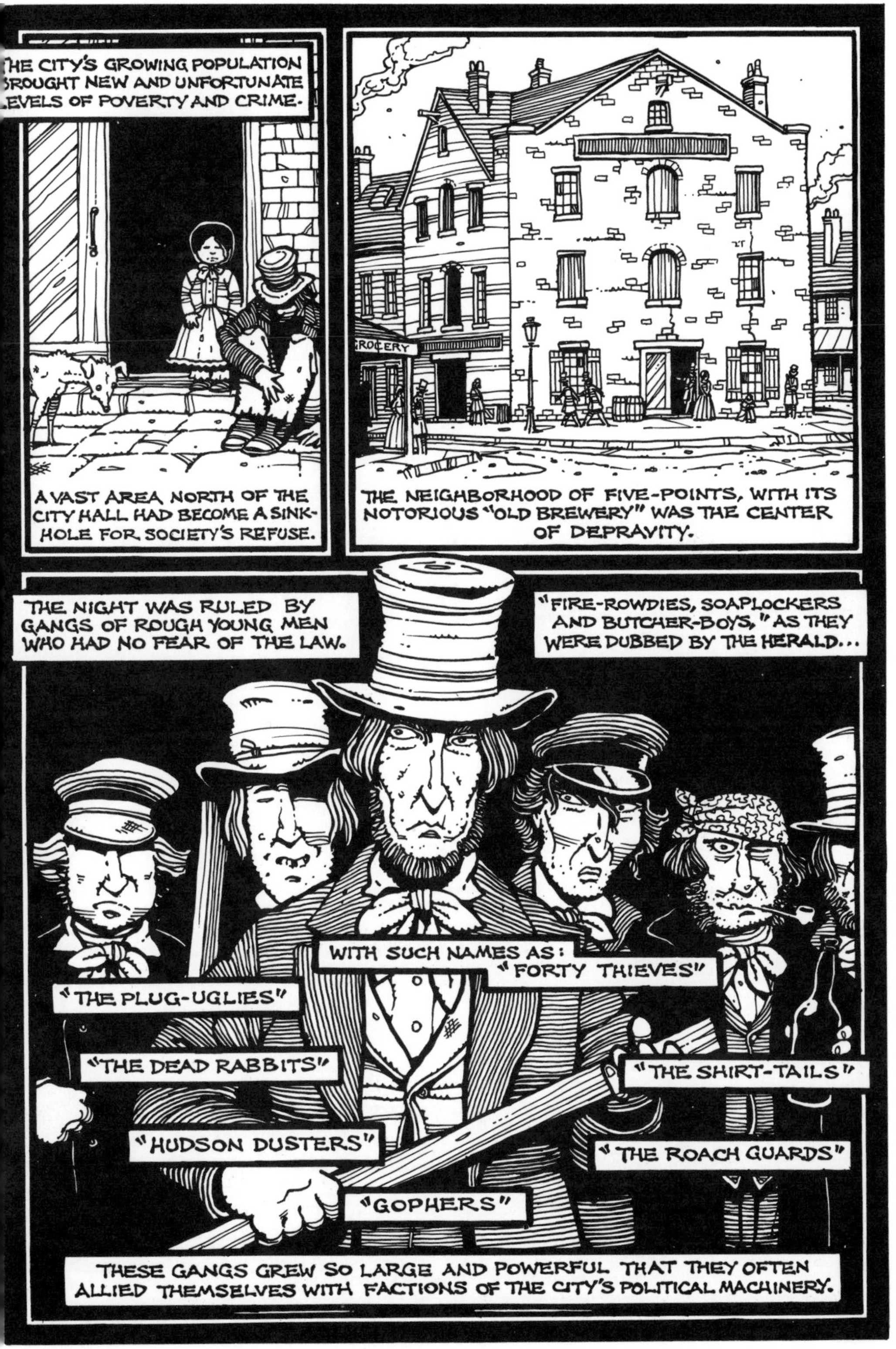

THE CITY'S GROWING POPULATION BROUGHT NEW AND UNFORTUNATE LEVELS OF POVERTY AND CRIME.
A VAST AREA NORTH OF THE CITY HALL HAD BECOME A SINK-HOLE FOR SOCIETY'S REFUSE.
GROCERY
THE NEIGHBORHOOD OF FIVE-POINTS, WITH ITS NOTORIOUS "OLD BREWERY" WAS THE CENTER OF DEPRAVITY.
THE NIGHT WAS RULED BY GANGS OF ROUGH YOUNG MEN WHO HAD NO FEAR OF THE LAW.
"FIRE-ROWDIES, SOAPLOCKERS AND BUTCHER-BOYS," AS THEY WERE DUBBED BY THE HERALD...
WITH SUCH NAMES AS:
"FORTY THIEVES"
"THE PLUG-UGLIES"
"THE DEAD RABBITS"
"THE SHIRT-TAILS"
"HUDSON DUSTERS"
"THE ROACH GUARDS"
"GOPHERS"
THESE GANGS GREW SO LARGE AND POWERFUL THAT THEY OFTEN ALLIED THEMSELVES WITH FACTIONS OF THE CITY'S POLITICAL MACHINERY.

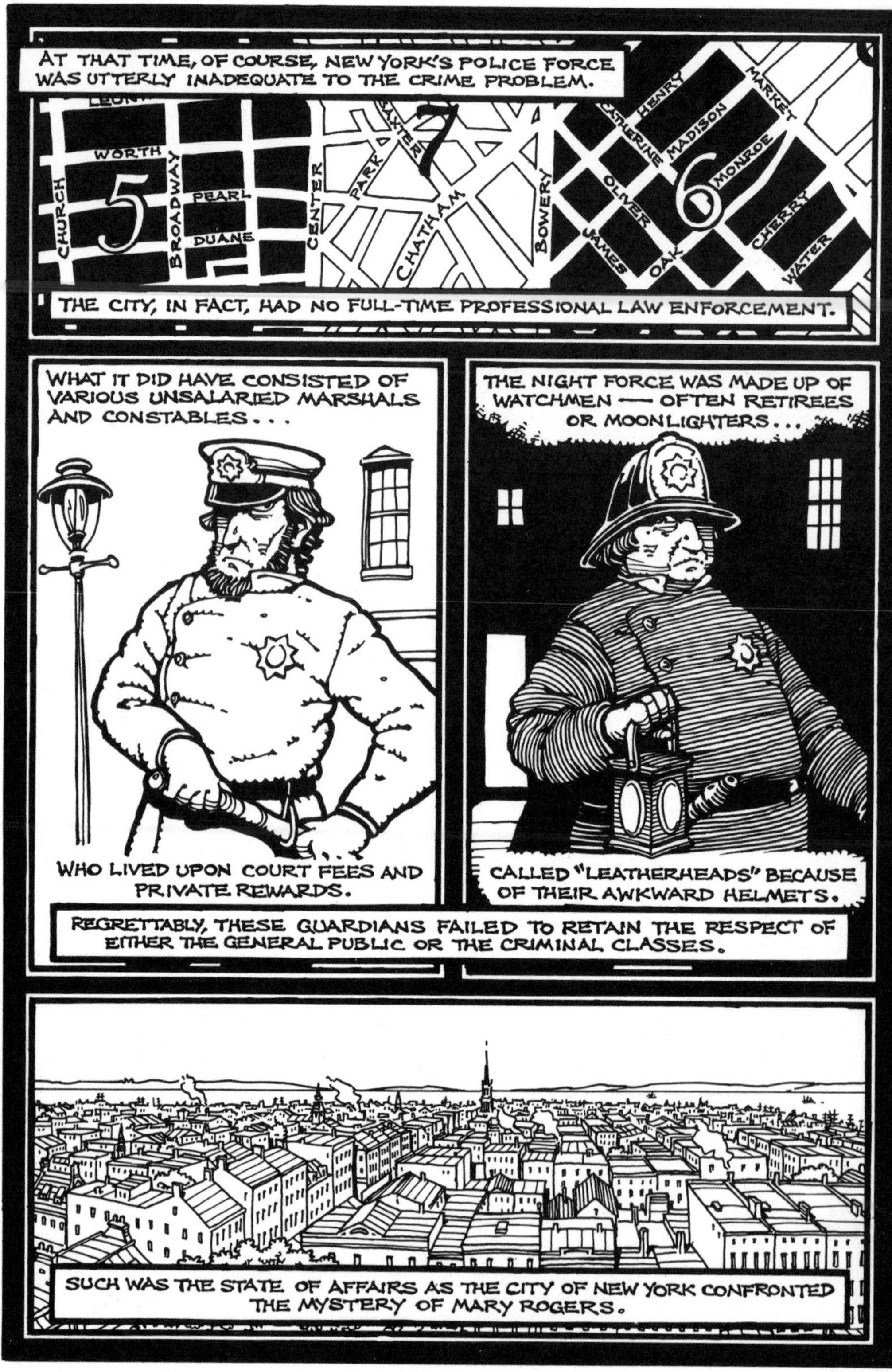
AT THAT TIME, OF COURSE, NEW YORK'S POLICE FORCE WAS UTTERLY INADEQUATE TO THE CRIME PROBLEM.
WORTH
CHURCH
5
BROADWAY
PEARL
DUANE
CENTER
PARK
BAXTER
7
CHATHAM
BOWERY
CATHERINE
HENRY
MADISON
MARKET
MONROE
6
OLIVER
JAMES
OAK
CHERRY
WATER
THE CITY, IN FACT, HAD NO FULL-TIME PROFESSIONAL LAW ENFORCEMENT.
WHAT IT DID HAVE CONSISTED OF VARIOUS UNSALARIED MARSHALS AND CONSTABLES...
WHO LIVED UPON COURT FEES AND PRIVATE REWARDS.
THE NIGHT FORCE WAS MADE UP OF WATCHMEN — OFTEN RETIREES OR MOONLIGHTERS...
CALLED "LEATHERHEADS" BECAUSE OF THEIR AWKWARD HELMETS.
REGRETTABLY, THESE GUARDIANS FAILED TO RETAIN THE RESPECT OF EITHER THE GENERAL PUBLIC OR THE CRIMINAL CLASSES.
SUCH WAS THE STATE OF AFFAIRS AS THE CITY OF NEW YORK CONFRONTED THE MYSTERY OF MARY ROGERS.

PART II.

THE HISTORY OF
MARY CECILIA ROGERS,
AND THE DAYS THAT LED
TO HER MURDER.

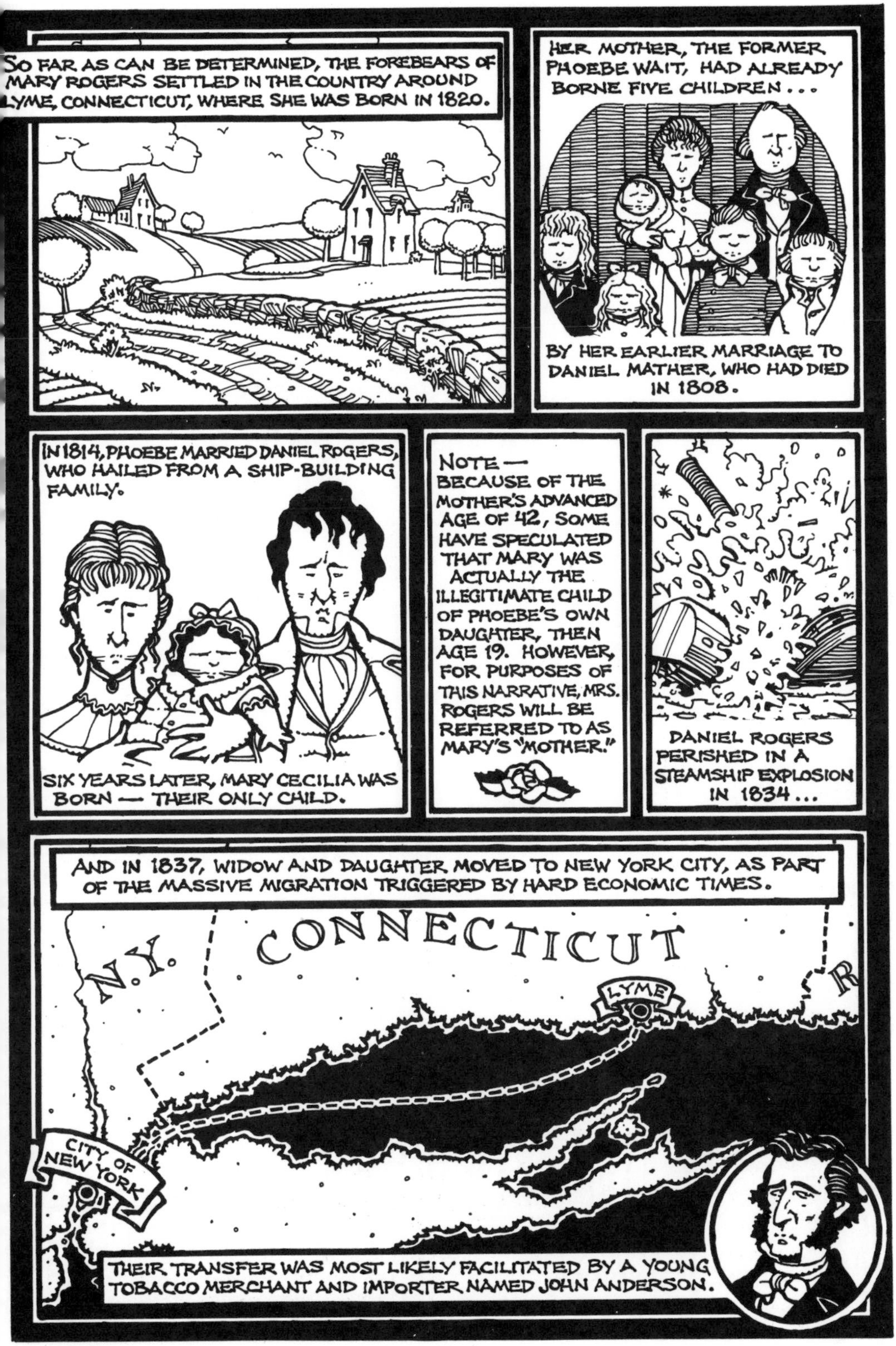

SO FAR AS CAN BE DETERMINED, THE FOREBEARS OF MARY ROGERS SETTLED IN THE COUNTRY AROUND LYME, CONNECTICUT, WHERE SHE WAS BORN IN 1820.
HER MOTHER, THE FORMER PHOEBE WAIT, HAD ALREADY BORNE FIVE CHILDREN . . .
BY HER EARLIER MARRIAGE TO DANIEL MATHER, WHO HAD DIED IN 1808.
IN 1814, PHOEBE MARRIED DANIEL ROGERS, WHO HAILED FROM A SHIP-BUILDING FAMILY.
SIX YEARS LATER, MARY CECILIA WAS BORN — THEIR ONLY CHILD.
NOTE — BECAUSE OF THE MOTHER'S ADVANCED AGE OF 42, SOME HAVE SPECULATED THAT MARY WAS ACTUALLY THE ILLEGITIMATE CHILD OF PHOEBE'S OWN DAUGHTER, THEN AGE 19. HOWEVER, FOR PURPOSES OF THIS NARRATIVE, MRS. ROGERS WILL BE REFERRED TO AS MARY'S "MOTHER."
DANIEL ROGERS PERISHED IN A STEAMSHIP EXPLOSION IN 1834 . . .
AND IN 1837, WIDOW AND DAUGHTER MOVED TO NEW YORK CITY, AS PART OF THE MASSIVE MIGRATION TRIGGERED BY HARD ECONOMIC TIMES.
N.Y.
CONNECTICUT
R
LYME
CITY OF NEW YORK
THEIR TRANSFER WAS MOST LIKELY FACILITATED BY A YOUNG TOBACCO MERCHANT AND IMPORTER NAMED JOHN ANDERSON.

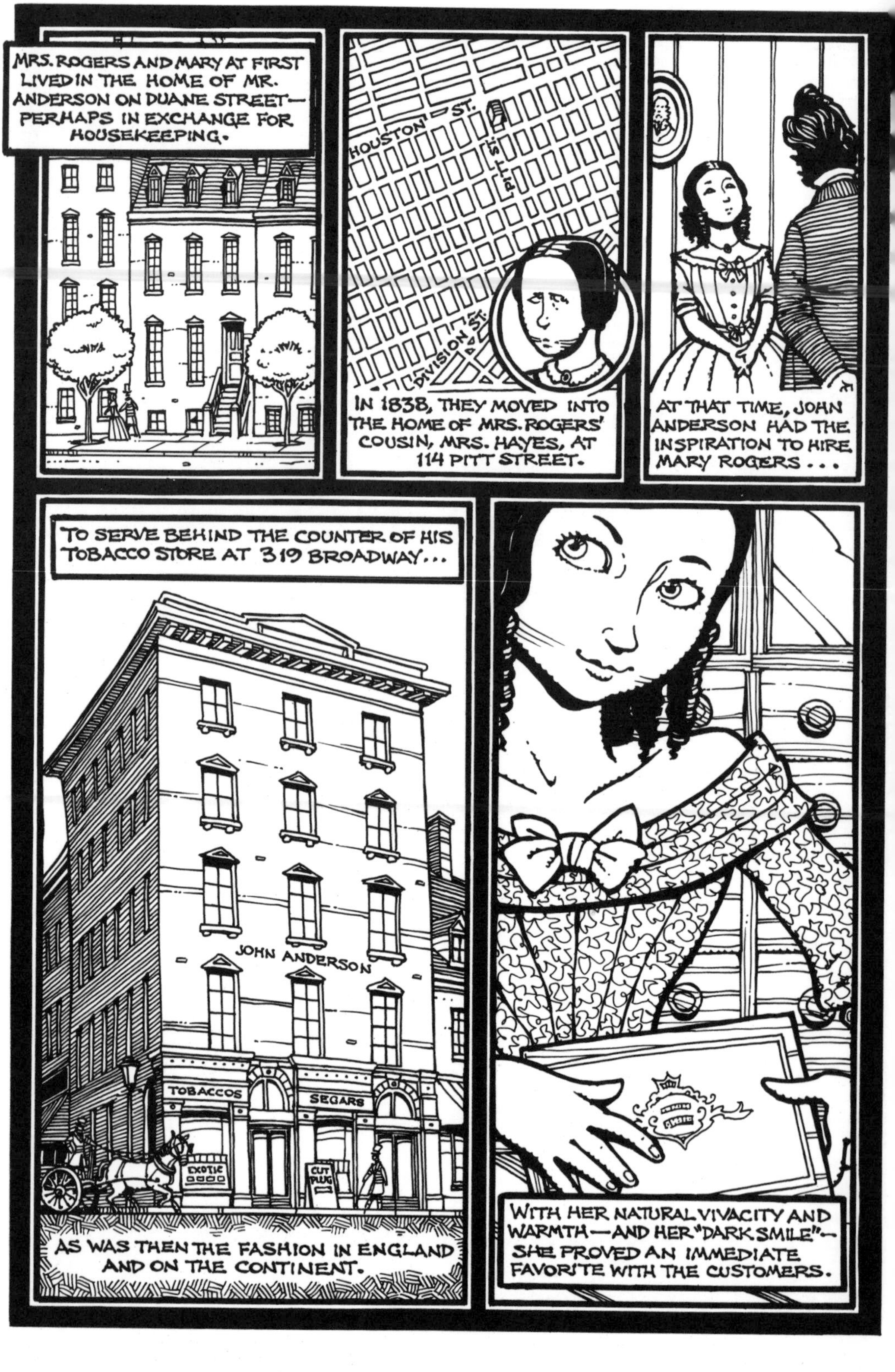
MRS. ROGERS AND MARY AT FIRST LIVED IN THE HOME OF MR. ANDERSON ON DUANE STREET— PERHAPS IN EXCHANGE FOR HOUSEKEEPING.
HOUSTON ST.
PITT ST.
DIVISION ST.
IN 1838, THEY MOVED INTO THE HOME OF MRS. ROGERS' COUSIN, MRS. HAYES, AT 114 PITT STREET.
AT THAT TIME, JOHN ANDERSON HAD THE INSPIRATION TO HIRE MARY ROGERS . . .
TO SERVE BEHIND THE COUNTER OF HIS TOBACCO STORE AT 319 BROADWAY...
JOHN ANDERSON
TOBACCOS
SEGARS
EXOTIC
CUT PLUG
AS WAS THEN THE FASHION IN ENGLAND AND ON THE CONTINENT.
WITH HER NATURAL VIVACITY AND WARMTH—AND HER "DARK SMILE"— SHE PROVED AN IMMEDIATE FAVORITE WITH THE CUSTOMERS.

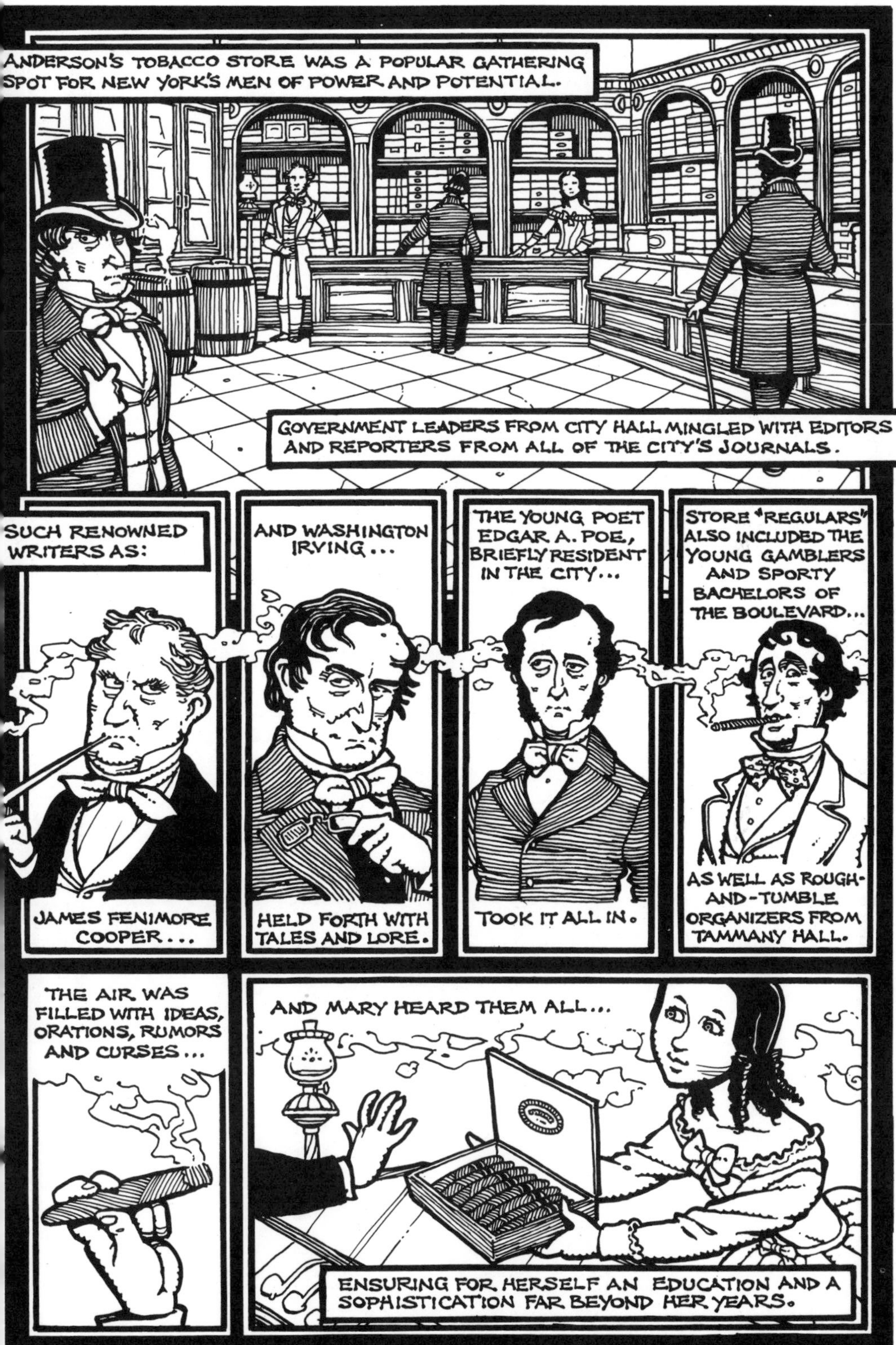
ANDERSON'S TOBACCO STORE WAS A POPULAR GATHERING SPOT FOR NEW YORK'S MEN OF POWER AND POTENTIAL.
GOVERNMENT LEADERS FROM CITY HALL MINGLED WITH EDITORS AND REPORTERS FROM ALL OF THE CITY'S JOURNALS.
SUCH RENOWNED WRITERS AS:
JAMES FENIMORE COOPER...
AND WASHINGTON IRVING...
HELD FORTH WITH TALES AND LORE.
THE YOUNG POET EDGAR A. POE, BRIEFLY RESIDENT IN THE CITY...
TOOK IT ALL IN.
STORE "REGULARS" ALSO INCLUDED THE YOUNG GAMBLERS AND SPORTY BACHELORS OF THE BOULEVARD...
AS WELL AS ROUGH-AND-TUMBLE ORGANIZERS FROM TAMMANY HALL.
THE AIR WAS FILLED WITH IDEAS, ORATIONS, RUMORS AND CURSES...
AND MARY HEARD THEM ALL...
ENSURING FOR HERSELF AN EDUCATION AND A SOPHISTICATION FAR BEYOND HER YEARS.

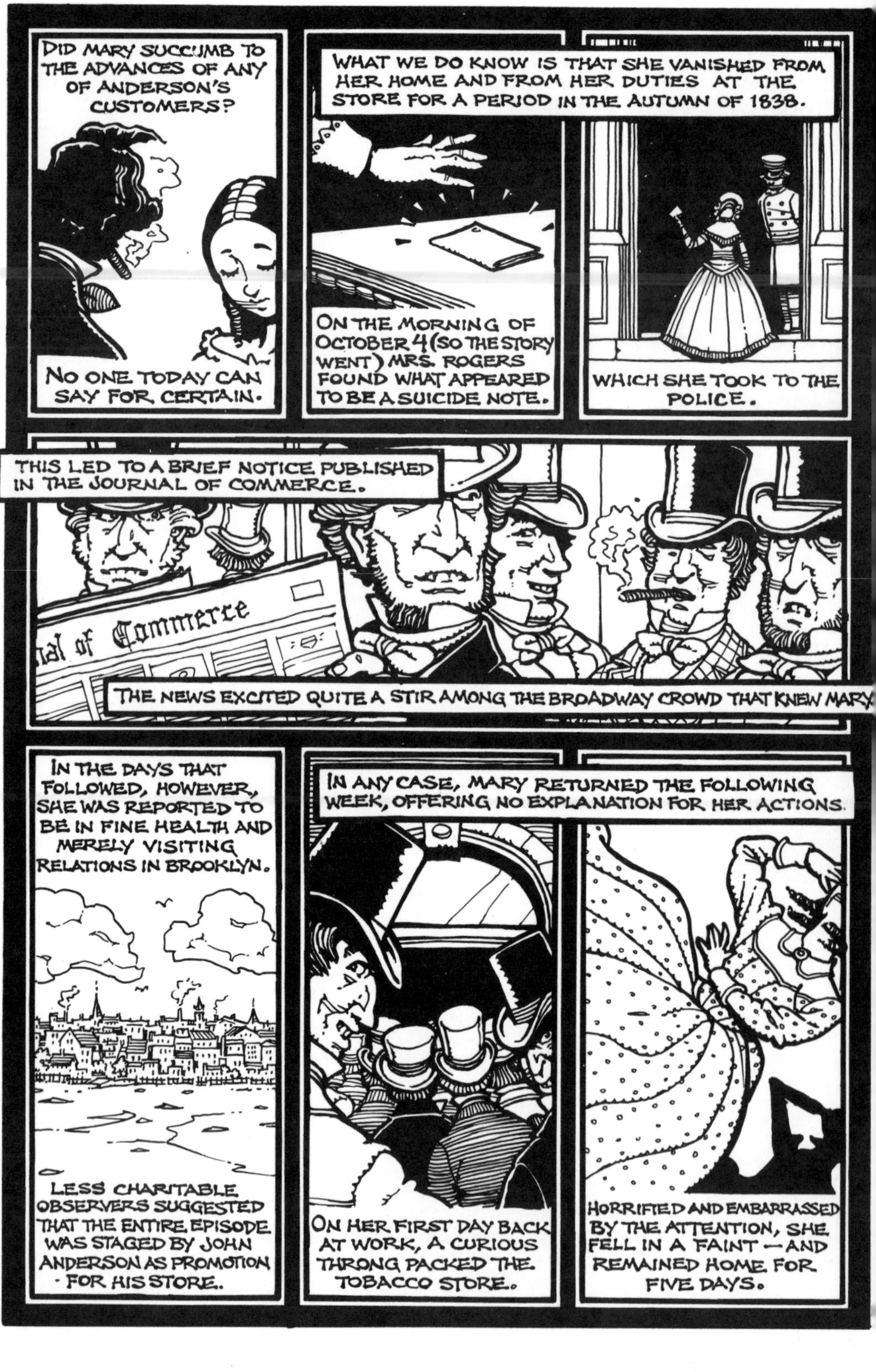
DID MARY SUCCUMB TO THE ADVANCES OF ANY OF ANDERSON'S CUSTOMERS?
NO ONE TODAY CAN SAY FOR CERTAIN.
WHAT WE DO KNOW IS THAT SHE VANISHED FROM HER HOME AND FROM HER DUTIES AT THE STORE FOR A PERIOD IN THE AUTUMN OF 1838.
ON THE MORNING OF OCTOBER 4 (SO THE STORY WENT) MRS. ROGERS FOUND WHAT APPEARED TO BE A SUICIDE NOTE.
WHICH SHE TOOK TO THE POLICE.
THIS LED TO A BRIEF NOTICE PUBLISHED IN THE JOURNAL OF COMMERCE.
nal of Commerce
THE NEWS EXCITED QUITE A STIR AMONG THE BROADWAY CROWD THAT KNEW MARY.
IN THE DAYS THAT FOLLOWED, HOWEVER, SHE WAS REPORTED TO BE IN FINE HEALTH AND MERELY VISITING RELATIONS IN BROOKLYN.
LESS CHARITABLE OBSERVERS SUGGESTED THAT THE ENTIRE EPISODE WAS STAGED BY JOHN ANDERSON AS PROMOTION FOR HIS STORE.
IN ANY CASE, MARY RETURNED THE FOLLOWING WEEK, OFFERING NO EXPLANATION FOR HER ACTIONS.
ON HER FIRST DAY BACK AT WORK, A CURIOUS THRONG PACKED THE TOBACCO STORE.
HORRIFIED AND EMBARRASSED BY THE ATTENTION, SHE FELL IN A FAINT — AND REMAINED HOME FOR FIVE DAYS.

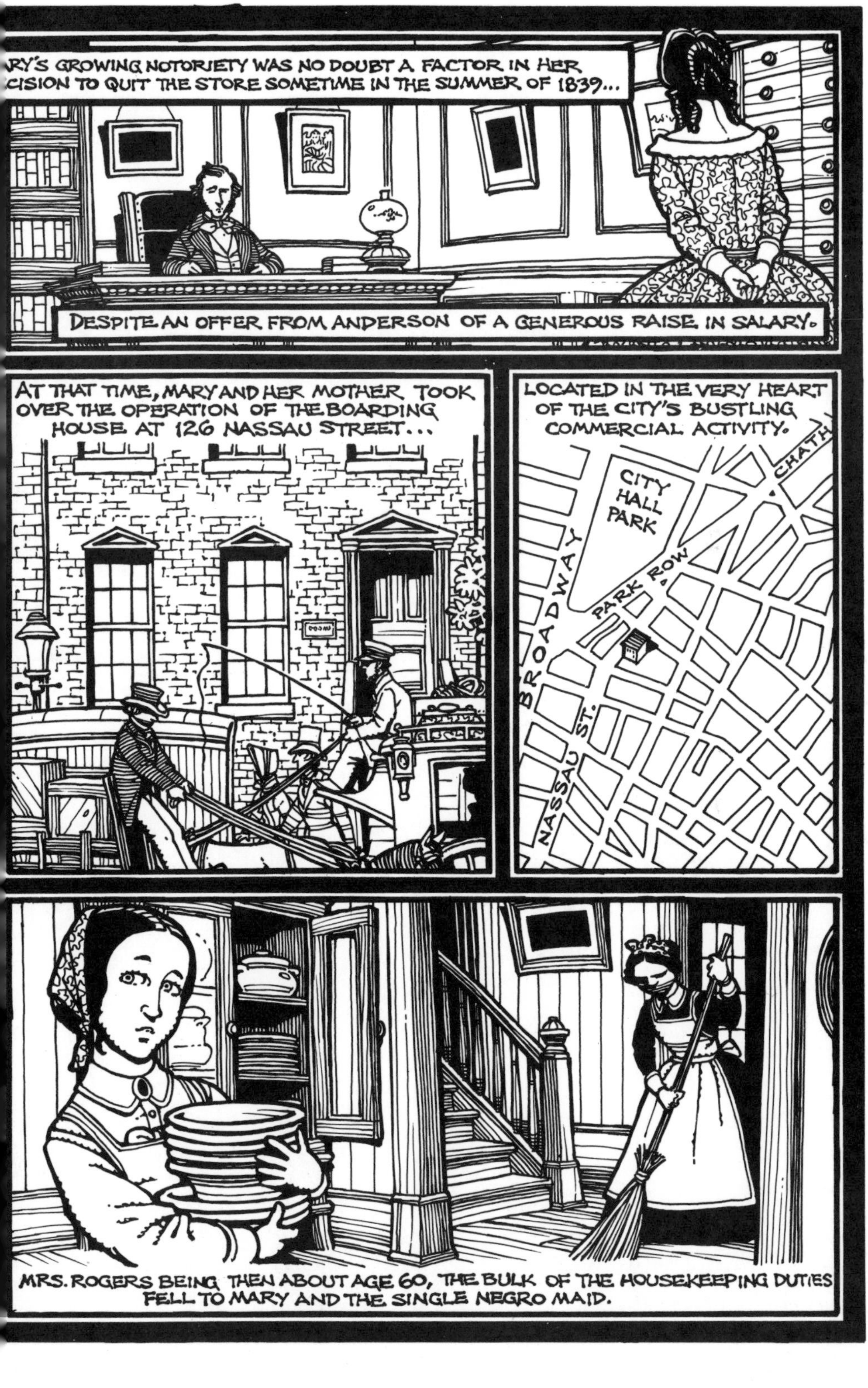

RY'S GROWING NOTORIETY WAS NO DOUBT A FACTOR IN HER
CISION TO QUIT THE STORE SOMETIME IN THE SUMMER OF 1839...
DESPITE AN OFFER FROM ANDERSON OF A GENEROUS RAISE IN SALARY.
AT THAT TIME, MARY AND HER MOTHER TOOK OVER THE OPERATION OF THE BOARDING HOUSE AT 126 NASSAU STREET...
LOCATED IN THE VERY HEART OF THE CITY'S BUSTLING COMMERCIAL ACTIVITY.
CITY HALL PARK
BROADWAY
PARK ROW
NASSAU ST.
CHATH
MRS. ROGERS BEING THEN ABOUT AGE 60, THE BULK OF THE HOUSEKEEPING DUTIES FELL TO MARY AND THE SINGLE NEGRO MAID.

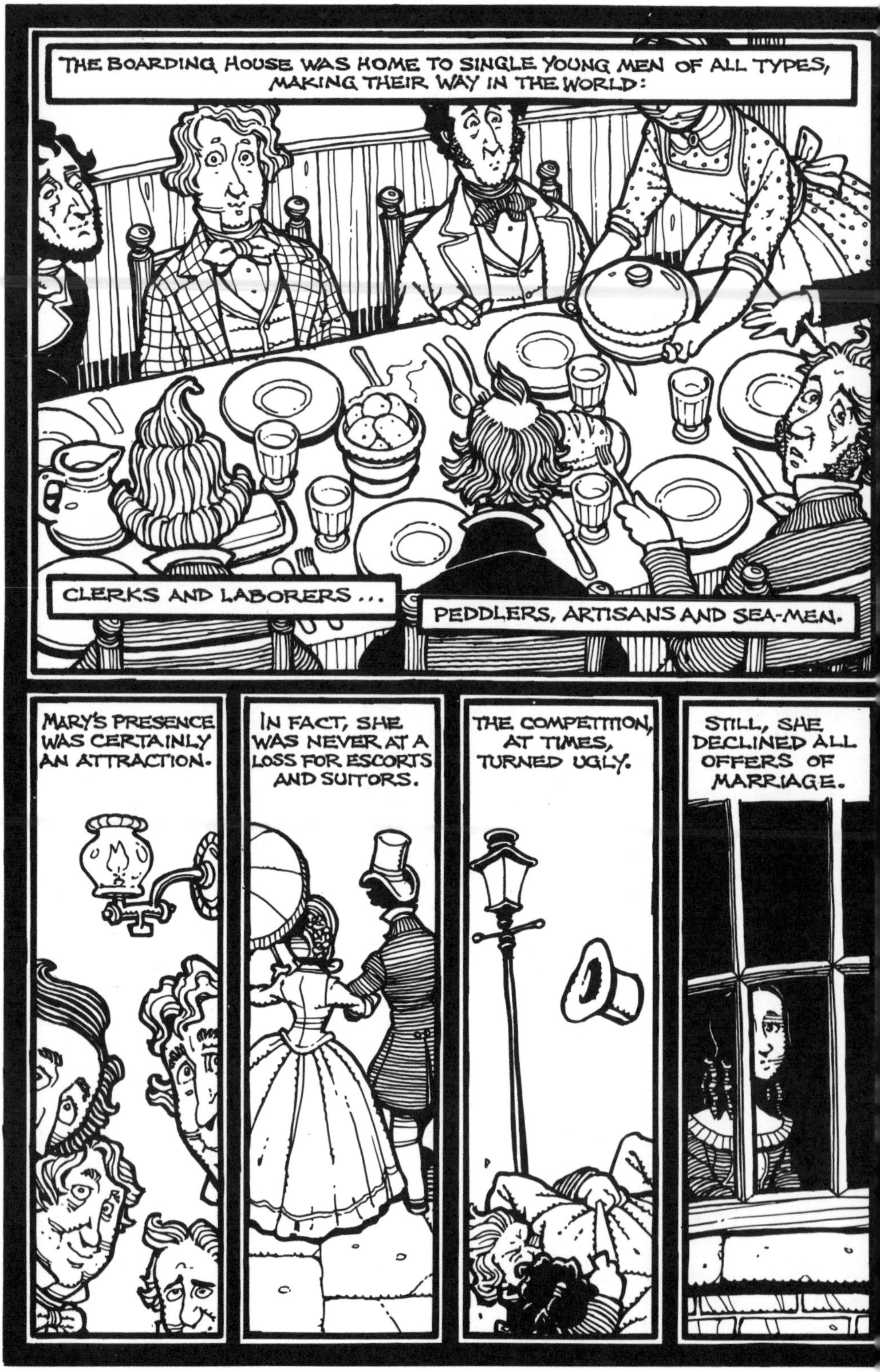
THE BOARDING HOUSE WAS HOME TO SINGLE YOUNG MEN OF ALL TYPES, MAKING THEIR WAY IN THE WORLD:
CLERKS AND LABORERS...
PEDDLERS, ARTISANS AND SEA-MEN.
MARY'S PRESENCE WAS CERTAINLY AN ATTRACTION.
IN FACT, SHE WAS NEVER AT A LOSS FOR ESCORTS AND SUITORS.
THE COMPETITION, AT TIMES, TURNED UGLY.
STILL, SHE DECLINED ALL OFFERS OF MARRIAGE.

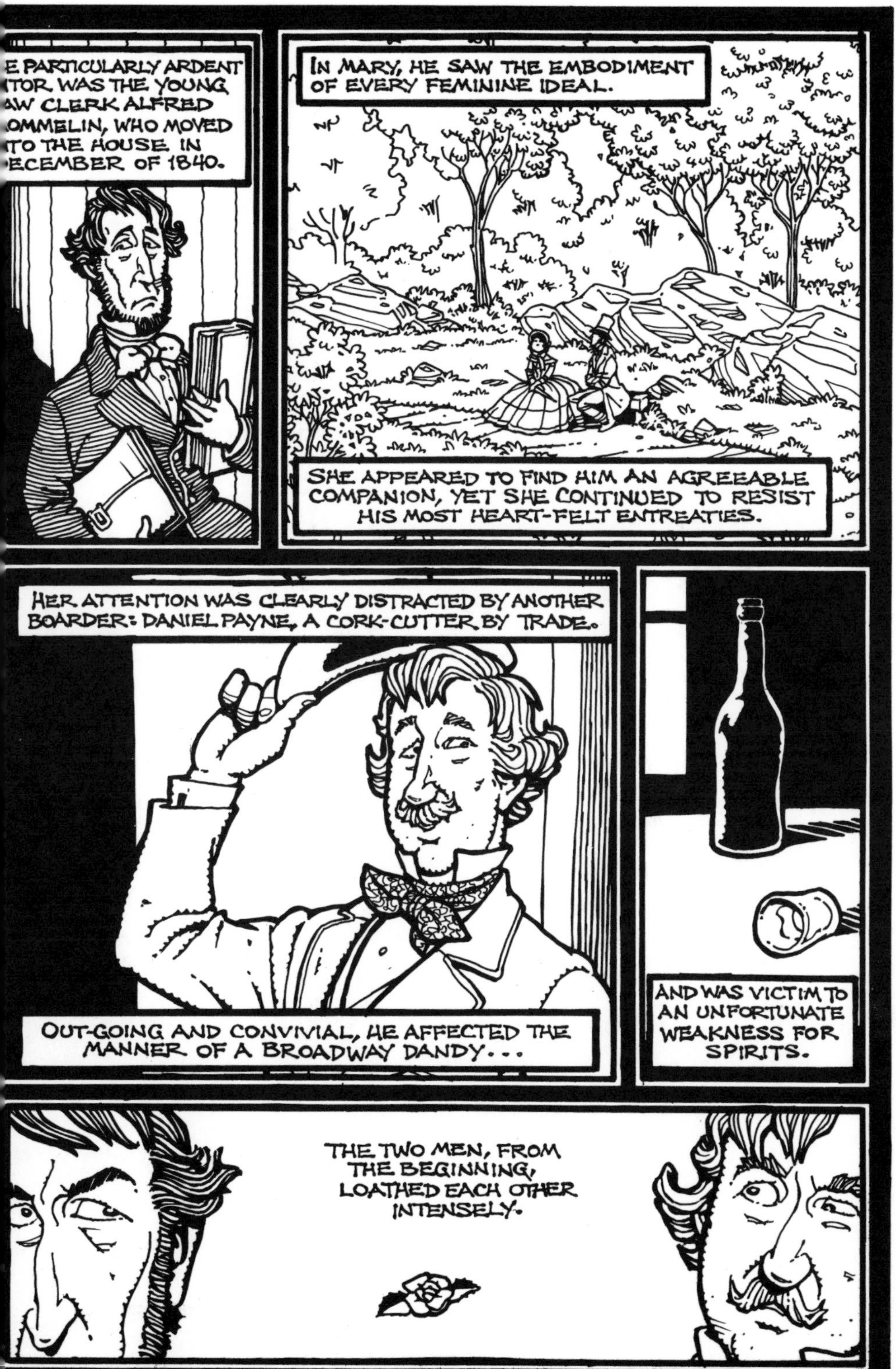
E PARTICULARLY ARDENT
ITOR WAS THE YOUNG
AW CLERK ALFRED
OMMELIN, WHO MOVED
TO THE HOUSE IN
ECEMBER OF 1840.
IN MARY, HE SAW THE EMBODIMENT OF EVERY FEMININE IDEAL.
SHE APPEARED TO FIND HIM AN AGREEABLE COMPANION, YET SHE CONTINUED TO RESIST HIS MOST HEART-FELT ENTREATIES.
HER ATTENTION WAS CLEARLY DISTRACTED BY ANOTHER BOARDER: DANIEL PAYNE, A CORK-CUTTER BY TRADE.
OUT-GOING AND CONVIVIAL, HE AFFECTED THE MANNER OF A BROADWAY DANDY...
AND WAS VICTIM TO AN UNFORTUNATE WEAKNESS FOR SPIRITS.
THE TWO MEN, FROM THE BEGINNING, LOATHED EACH OTHER INTENSELY.

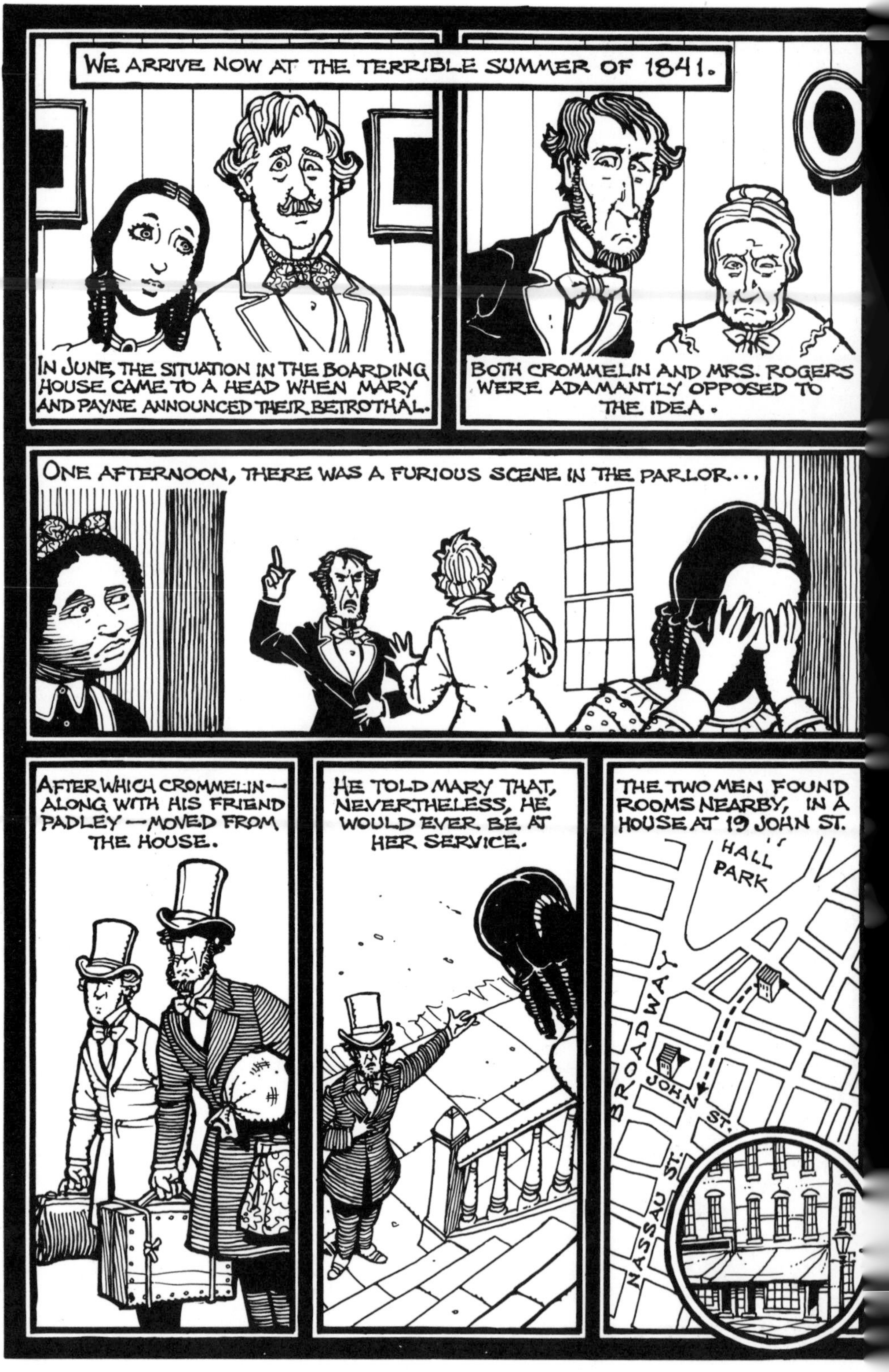
WE ARRIVE NOW AT THE TERRIBLE SUMMER OF 1841.
IN JUNE, THE SITUATION IN THE BOARDING HOUSE CAME TO A HEAD WHEN MARY AND PAYNE ANNOUNCED THEIR BETROTHAL.
BOTH CROMMELIN AND MRS. ROGERS WERE ADAMANTLY OPPOSED TO THE IDEA.
ONE AFTERNOON, THERE WAS A FURIOUS SCENE IN THE PARLOR...
AFTER WHICH CROMMELIN— ALONG WITH HIS FRIEND PADLEY —MOVED FROM THE HOUSE.
HE TOLD MARY THAT, NEVERTHELESS, HE WOULD EVER BE AT HER SERVICE.
THE TWO MEN FOUND ROOMS NEARBY, IN A HOUSE AT 19 JOHN ST.
HALL
PARK
BROADWAY
JOHN ST.
NASSAU ST.

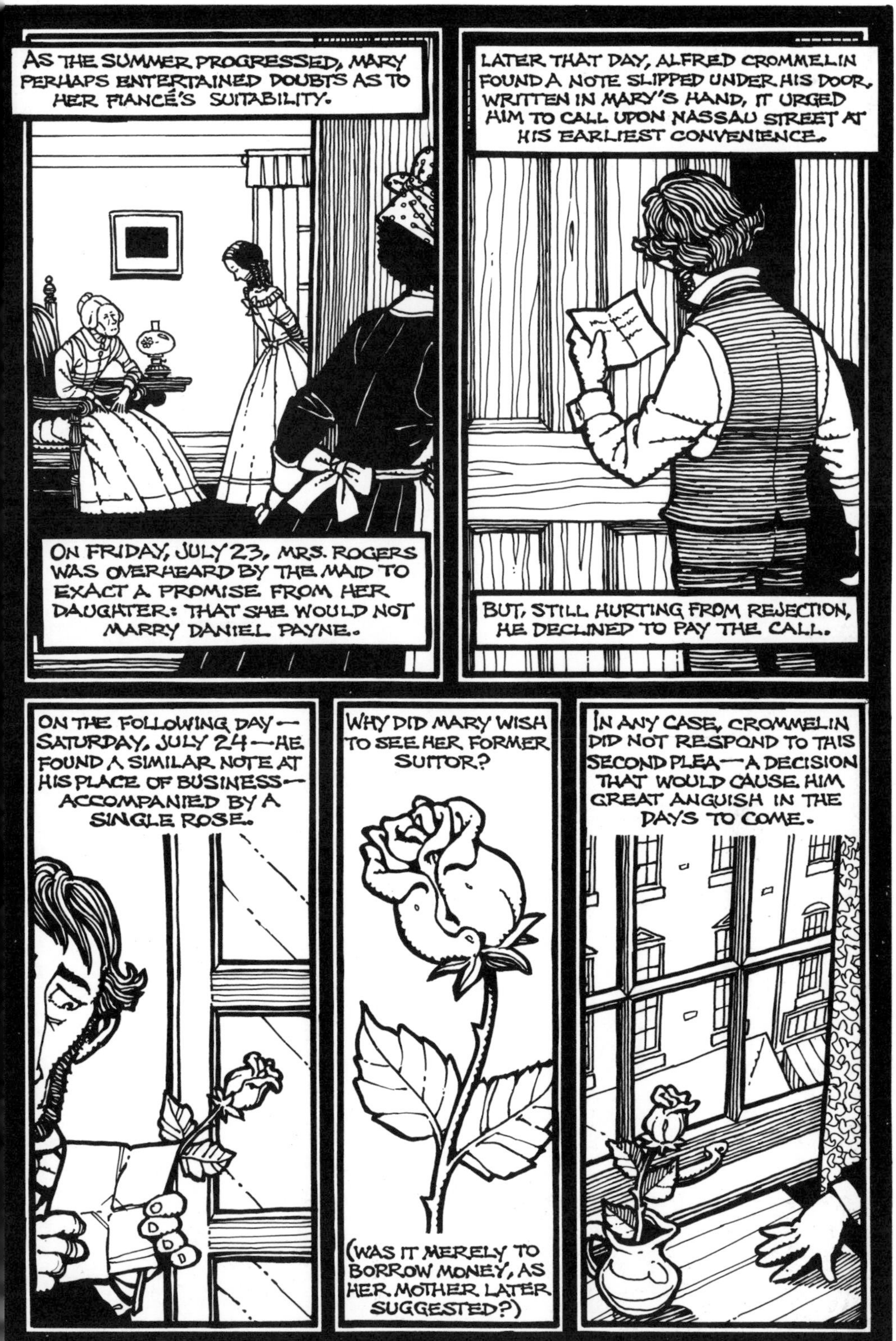
AS THE SUMMER PROGRESSED, MARY PERHAPS ENTERTAINED DOUBTS AS TO HER FIANCÉ'S SUITABILITY.
ON FRIDAY, JULY 23, MRS. ROGERS WAS OVERHEARD BY THE MAID TO EXACT A PROMISE FROM HER DAUGHTER: THAT SHE WOULD NOT MARRY DANIEL PAYNE.
LATER THAT DAY, ALFRED CROMMELIN FOUND A NOTE SLIPPED UNDER HIS DOOR. WRITTEN IN MARY'S HAND, IT URGED HIM TO CALL UPON NASSAU STREET AT HIS EARLIEST CONVENIENCE.
BUT, STILL HURTING FROM REJECTION, HE DECLINED TO PAY THE CALL.
ON THE FOLLOWING DAY— SATURDAY, JULY 24—HE FOUND A SIMILAR NOTE AT HIS PLACE OF BUSINESS— ACCOMPANIED BY A SINGLE ROSE.
WHY DID MARY WISH TO SEE HER FORMER SUITOR?
(WAS IT MERELY TO BORROW MONEY, AS HER MOTHER LATER SUGGESTED?)
IN ANY CASE, CROMMELIN DID NOT RESPOND TO THIS SECOND PLEA—A DECISION THAT WOULD CAUSE HIM GREAT ANGUISH IN THE DAYS TO COME.

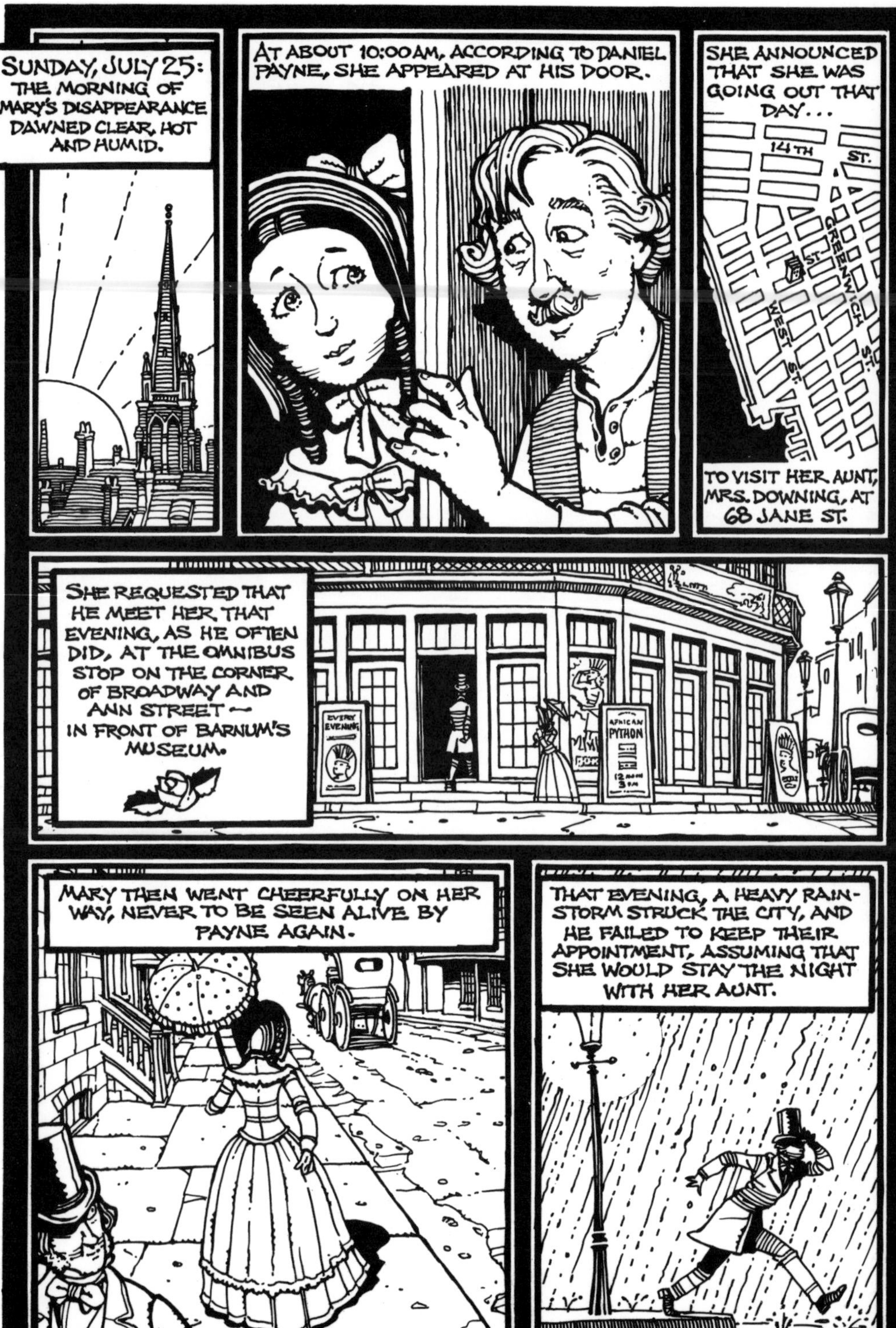
SUNDAY, JULY 25: THE MORNING OF MARY'S DISAPPEARANCE DAWNED CLEAR, HOT AND HUMID.
AT ABOUT 10:00 AM, ACCORDING TO DANIEL PAYNE, SHE APPEARED AT HIS DOOR.
SHE ANNOUNCED THAT SHE WAS GOING OUT THAT DAY...
14TH ST.
GREENWICH ST.
WEST ST.
TO VISIT HER AUNT, MRS. DOWNING, AT 68 JANE ST.
SHE REQUESTED THAT HE MEET HER THAT EVENING, AS HE OFTEN DID, AT THE OMNIBUS STOP ON THE CORNER OF BROADWAY AND ANN STREET — IN FRONT OF BARNUM'S MUSEUM.
EVERY EVENING
AFRICAN PYTHON
MARY THEN WENT CHEERFULLY ON HER WAY, NEVER TO BE SEEN ALIVE BY PAYNE AGAIN.
THAT EVENING, A HEAVY RAIN-STORM STRUCK THE CITY, AND HE FAILED TO KEEP THEIR APPOINTMENT, ASSUMING THAT SHE WOULD STAY THE NIGHT WITH HER AUNT.

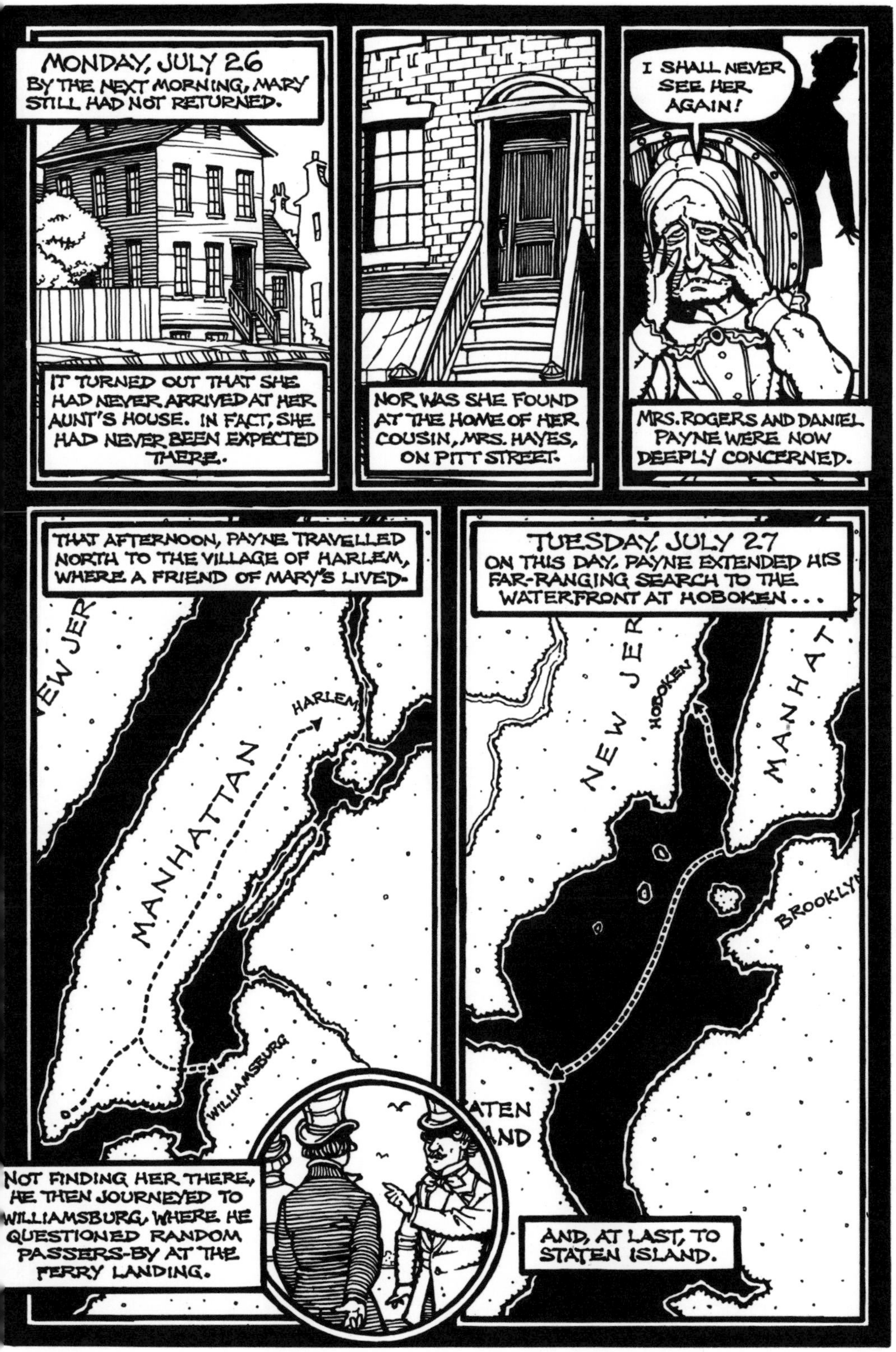
MONDAY, JULY 26
BY THE NEXT MORNING, MARY STILL HAD NOT RETURNED.
IT TURNED OUT THAT SHE HAD NEVER ARRIVED AT HER AUNT'S HOUSE. IN FACT, SHE HAD NEVER BEEN EXPECTED THERE.
NOR WAS SHE FOUND AT THE HOME OF HER COUSIN, MRS. HAYES, ON PITT STREET.
I SHALL NEVER SEE HER AGAIN!
MRS. ROGERS AND DANIEL PAYNE WERE NOW DEEPLY CONCERNED.
THAT AFTERNOON, PAYNE TRAVELLED NORTH TO THE VILLAGE OF HARLEM, WHERE A FRIEND OF MARY'S LIVED.
NEW JER
MANHATTAN
HARLEM
WILLIAMSBURG
NOT FINDING HER THERE, HE THEN JOURNEYED TO WILLIAMSBURG, WHERE HE QUESTIONED RANDOM PASSERS-BY AT THE FERRY LANDING.
TUESDAY, JULY 27
ON THIS DAY, PAYNE EXTENDED HIS FAR-RANGING SEARCH TO THE WATERFRONT AT HOBOKEN...
NEW JER
HOBOKEN
MANHAT
BROOKLYN
ATEN
AND
AND, AT LAST, TO STATEN ISLAND.

THAT AFTERNOON, PAYNE VISITED THE OFFICES OF THE SUN, AND PLACED A "MISSING PERSONS" NOTICE:

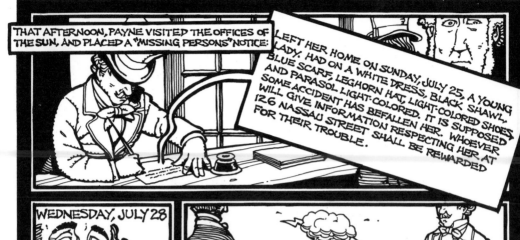

LEFT HER HOME ON SUNDAY, JULY 25, A YOUNG LADY. HAD ON A WHITE DRESS, BLACK SHAWL, BLUE SCARF, LEGHORN HAT, LIGHT-COLORED SHOES AND PARASOL LIGHT-COLORED. IT IS SUPPOSED SOME ACCIDENT HAS BEFALLEN HER. WHOEVER WILL GIVE INFORMATION RESPECTING HER AT 126 NASSAU STREET SHALL BE REWARDED FOR THEIR TROUBLE.

WEDNESDAY, JULY 28

WHEN ALFRED CROMMELIN READ THE NOTICE THAT MORNING, HE WENT AT ONCE TO NASSAU STREET.

THERE, HE ENCOUNTERED PAYNE FOR A TENSE MOMENT IN THE PARLOR.

PAYNE THEN WENT OUT TO CONTINUE HIS SEARCH: AT NOON, HE JOURNEYED AGAIN TO HOBOKEN ...

WHERE HE WALKED ALONG THE PATH TO THE SYBIL'S CAVE.

CROMMELIN, IN THE MEANTIME, PURSUED HIS OWN COURSE OF ACTION ...

FIRST, TO POLICE HEADQUARTERS IN A FRUITLESS EFFORT TO LOCATE THE HIGH CONSTABLE, JACOB HAYES.

THEN, WITH HIS FRIEND PADLEY, HE TOOK THE FERRY TO HOBOKEN (ARRIVING, IT SEEMED, ONLY MINUTES AFTER PAYNE'S DEPARTURE).

WHAT WAS IT THAT COMPELLED BOTH MEN THAT DAY TO SEEK THE LOST GIRL ON THE SHORES OF THE HUDSON AT HOBOKEN?

LATER THAT DAY, AS WE HAVE SEEN, MARY'S POOR BODY WAS RECOVERED FROM THE RIVER.

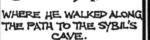

IT TOOK MUCH LONGER TO INITIATE AN INVESTIGATION INTO HER MURDER.

PART III.

THE INVESTIGATION

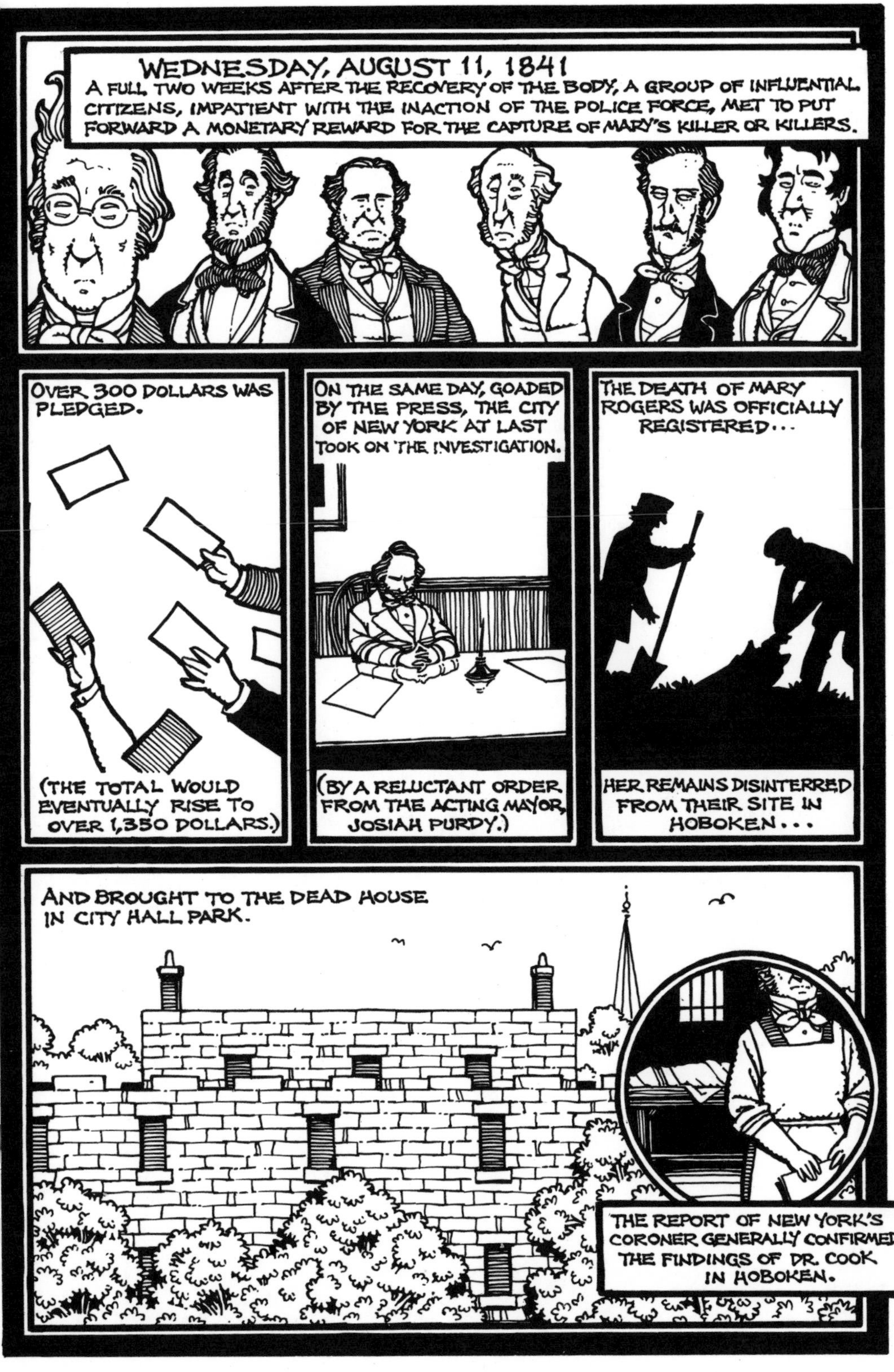

WEDNESDAY, AUGUST 11, 1841
A FULL TWO WEEKS AFTER THE RECOVERY OF THE BODY, A GROUP OF INFLUENTIAL CITIZENS, IMPATIENT WITH THE INACTION OF THE POLICE FORCE, MET TO PUT FORWARD A MONETARY REWARD FOR THE CAPTURE OF MARY'S KILLER OR KILLERS.
OVER 300 DOLLARS WAS PLEDGED.
(THE TOTAL WOULD EVENTUALLY RISE TO OVER 1,350 DOLLARS.)
ON THE SAME DAY, GOADED BY THE PRESS, THE CITY OF NEW YORK AT LAST TOOK ON THE INVESTIGATION.
(BY A RELUCTANT ORDER FROM THE ACTING MAYOR, JOSIAH PURDY.)
THE DEATH OF MARY ROGERS WAS OFFICIALLY REGISTERED...
HER REMAINS DISINTERRED FROM THEIR SITE IN HOBOKEN...
AND BROUGHT TO THE DEAD HOUSE IN CITY HALL PARK.
THE REPORT OF NEW YORK'S CORONER GENERALLY CONFIRMED THE FINDINGS OF DR. COOK IN HOBOKEN.

THURSDAY, AUGUST 12
DANIEL PAYNE, ALONG WITH MRS. ROGERS, MRS. HAYES, AND A GIRL-FRIEND OF MARY'S, WERE BROUGHT IN TO MAKE THE OFFICIAL IDENTIFICATION.

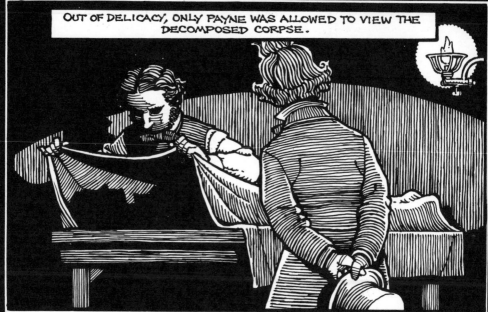

OUT OF DELICACY, ONLY PAYNE WAS ALLOWED TO VIEW THE DECOMPOSED CORPSE.

SADLY, HE RECOGNIZED THE FORM OF HIS DEPARTED LOVE.

THE LADIES, FOR THEIR PART, IDENTIFIED FURTHER ARTICLES OF APPAREL.

LATER THAT DAY, PAYNE WAS QUESTIONED BY POLICE SERGEANT McARDLE AS TO HIS MOVEMENTS ON THE SUNDAY OF MARY'S DISAPPEARANCE.

THIS WAS HIS STATEMENT:

AFTER BIDDING MARY GOODBYE AT 10:00 AM, HE COMPLETED HIS TOILET, CONSUMED BREAKFAST AND LEFT THE HOUSE AT 11:00 AM.

HE WALKED TO THE HOME OF HIS BROTHER, JOHN PAYNE AT 33 WARREN ST.

THE TWO OF THEM STROLLED DOWN BROADWAY, AND BROWSED AT SCOTT'S BAZAAR ON DEY STREET.

THEY PARTED IN FRONT OF ST. PAUL'S CHAPEL.

DANIEL PAYNE INDULGED HIMSELF TO A DRINK AT BICKFORD'S TAVERN ON JAMES STREET...

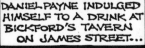

AND DINED AT GOSLIN'S RESTAURANT ON FULTON STREET.

HE THEN RETURNED TO THE BOARDING HOUSE FOR A THREE-HOUR SLUMBER.

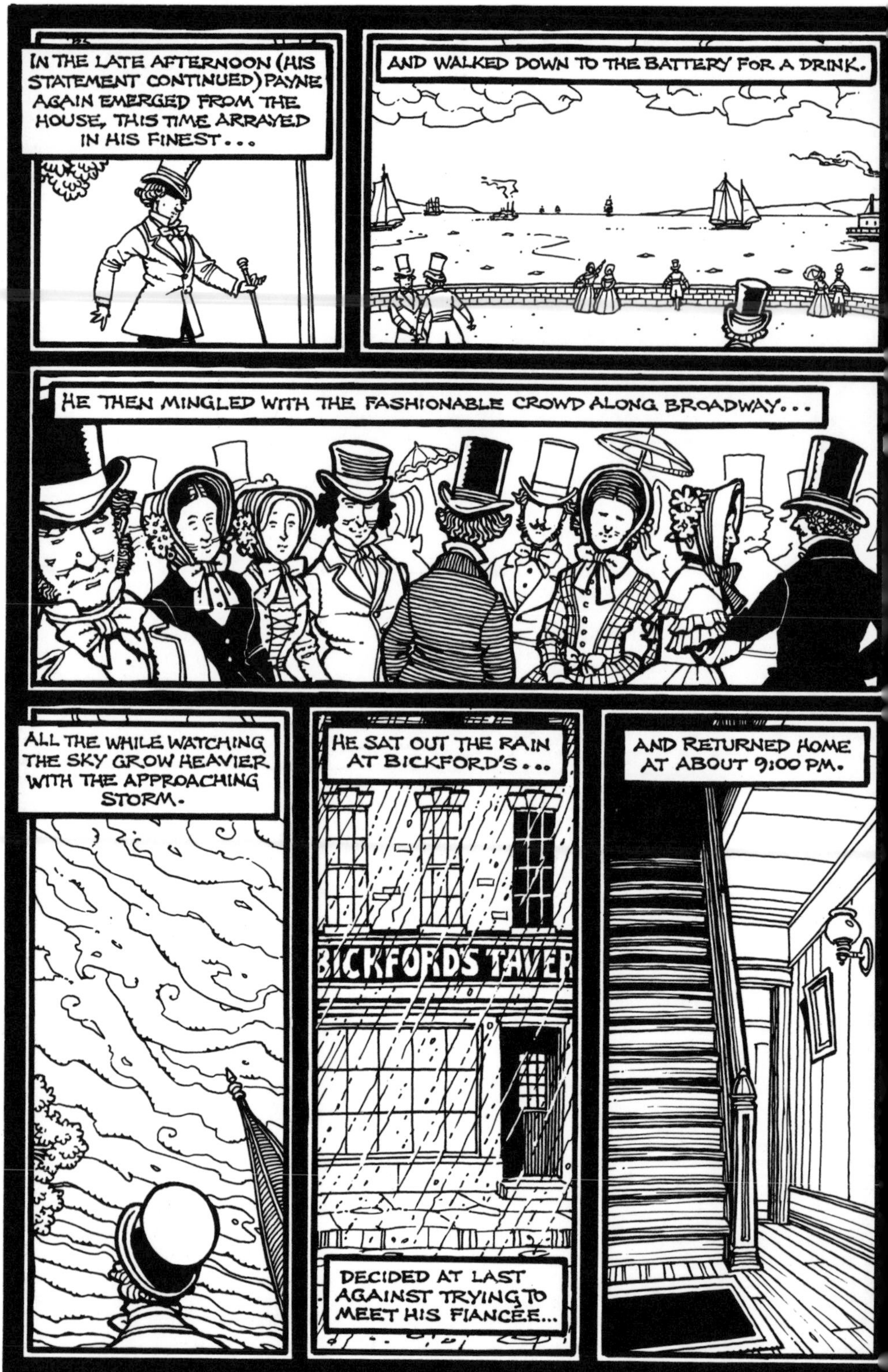
IN THE LATE AFTERNOON (HIS STATEMENT CONTINUED) PAYNE AGAIN EMERGED FROM THE HOUSE, THIS TIME ARRAYED IN HIS FINEST...
AND WALKED DOWN TO THE BATTERY FOR A DRINK.
HE THEN MINGLED WITH THE FASHIONABLE CROWD ALONG BROADWAY...
ALL THE WHILE WATCHING THE SKY GROW HEAVIER WITH THE APPROACHING STORM.
HE SAT OUT THE RAIN AT BICKFORD'S...
BICKFORD'S TAVER
DECIDED AT LAST AGAINST TRYING TO MEET HIS FIANCÉE...
AND RETURNED HOME AT ABOUT 9:00 PM.

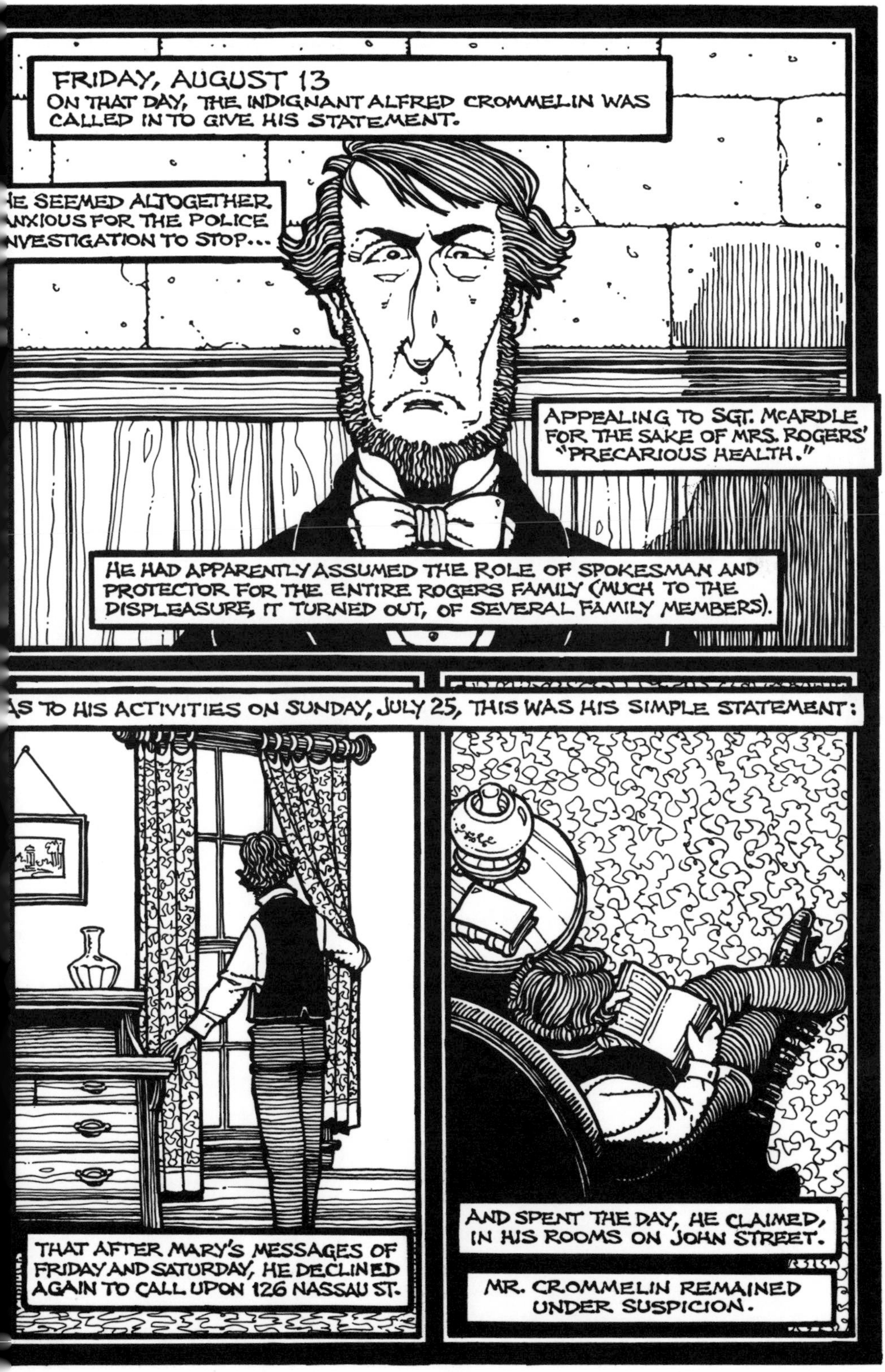
FRIDAY, AUGUST 13
ON THAT DAY, THE INDIGNANT ALFRED CROMMELIN WAS CALLED IN TO GIVE HIS STATEMENT.
HE SEEMED ALTOGETHER ANXIOUS FOR THE POLICE INVESTIGATION TO STOP...
APPEALING TO SGT. MCARDLE FOR THE SAKE OF MRS. ROGERS' "PRECARIOUS HEALTH."
HE HAD APPARENTLY ASSUMED THE ROLE OF SPOKESMAN AND PROTECTOR FOR THE ENTIRE ROGERS FAMILY (MUCH TO THE DISPLEASURE, IT TURNED OUT, OF SEVERAL FAMILY MEMBERS).
AS TO HIS ACTIVITIES ON SUNDAY, JULY 25, THIS WAS HIS SIMPLE STATEMENT:
THAT AFTER MARY'S MESSAGES OF FRIDAY AND SATURDAY, HE DECLINED AGAIN TO CALL UPON 126 NASSAU ST.
AND SPENT THE DAY, HE CLAIMED, IN HIS ROOMS ON JOHN STREET.
MR. CROMMELIN REMAINED UNDER SUSPICION.

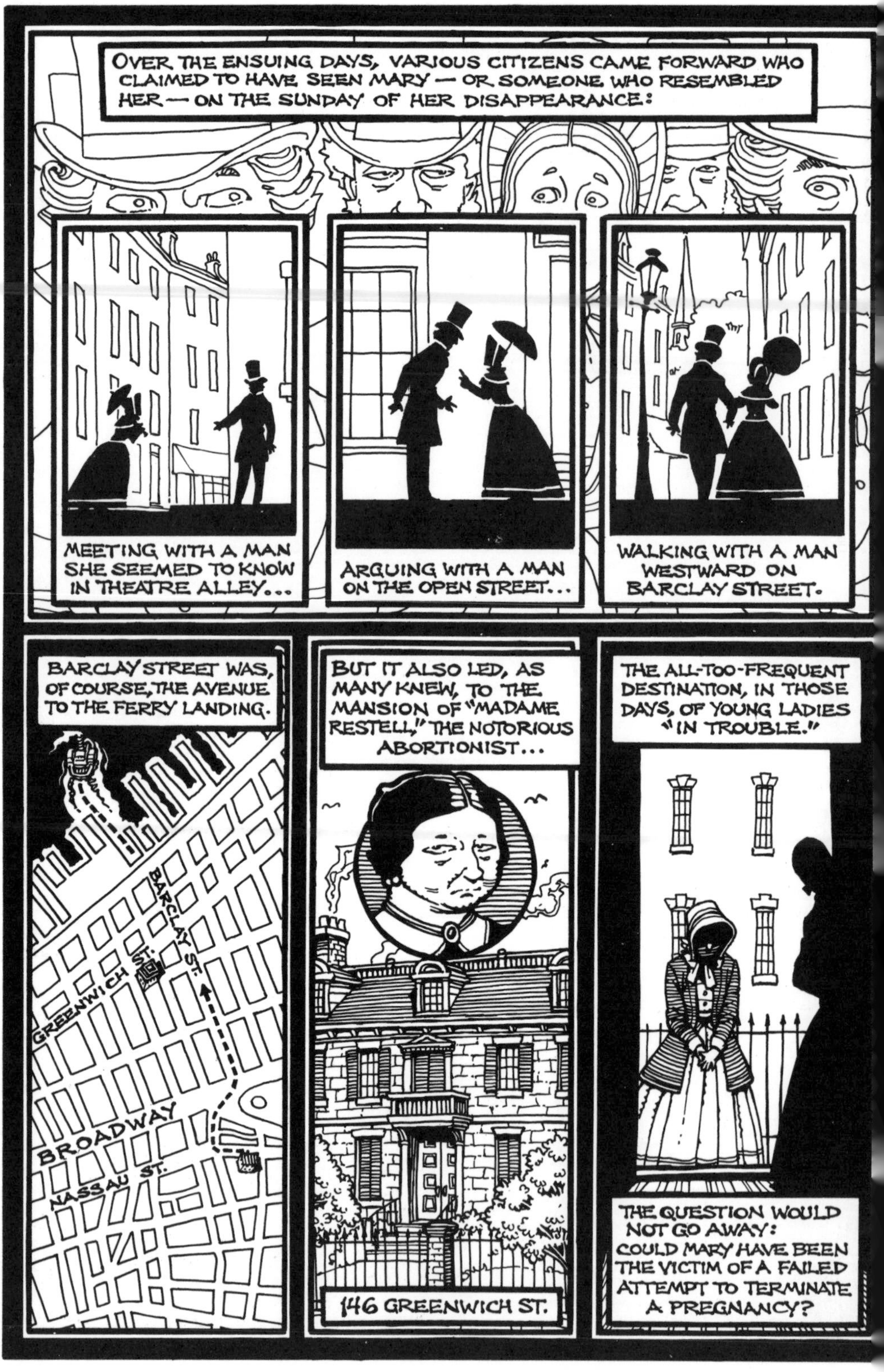

OVER THE ENSUING DAYS, VARIOUS CITIZENS CAME FORWARD WHO CLAIMED TO HAVE SEEN MARY — OR SOMEONE WHO RESEMBLED HER — ON THE SUNDAY OF HER DISAPPEARANCE:
MEETING WITH A MAN SHE SEEMED TO KNOW IN THEATRE ALLEY...
ARGUING WITH A MAN ON THE OPEN STREET...
WALKING WITH A MAN WESTWARD ON BARCLAY STREET.
BARCLAY STREET WAS, OF COURSE, THE AVENUE TO THE FERRY LANDING.
BARCLAY ST.
GREENWICH ST.
BROADWAY
NASSAU ST.
BUT IT ALSO LED, AS MANY KNEW, TO THE MANSION OF "MADAME RESTELL," THE NOTORIOUS ABORTIONIST...
146 GREENWICH ST.
THE ALL-TOO-FREQUENT DESTINATION, IN THOSE DAYS, OF YOUNG LADIES "IN TROUBLE."
THE QUESTION WOULD NOT GO AWAY: COULD MARY HAVE BEEN THE VICTIM OF A FAILED ATTEMPT TO TERMINATE A PREGNANCY?

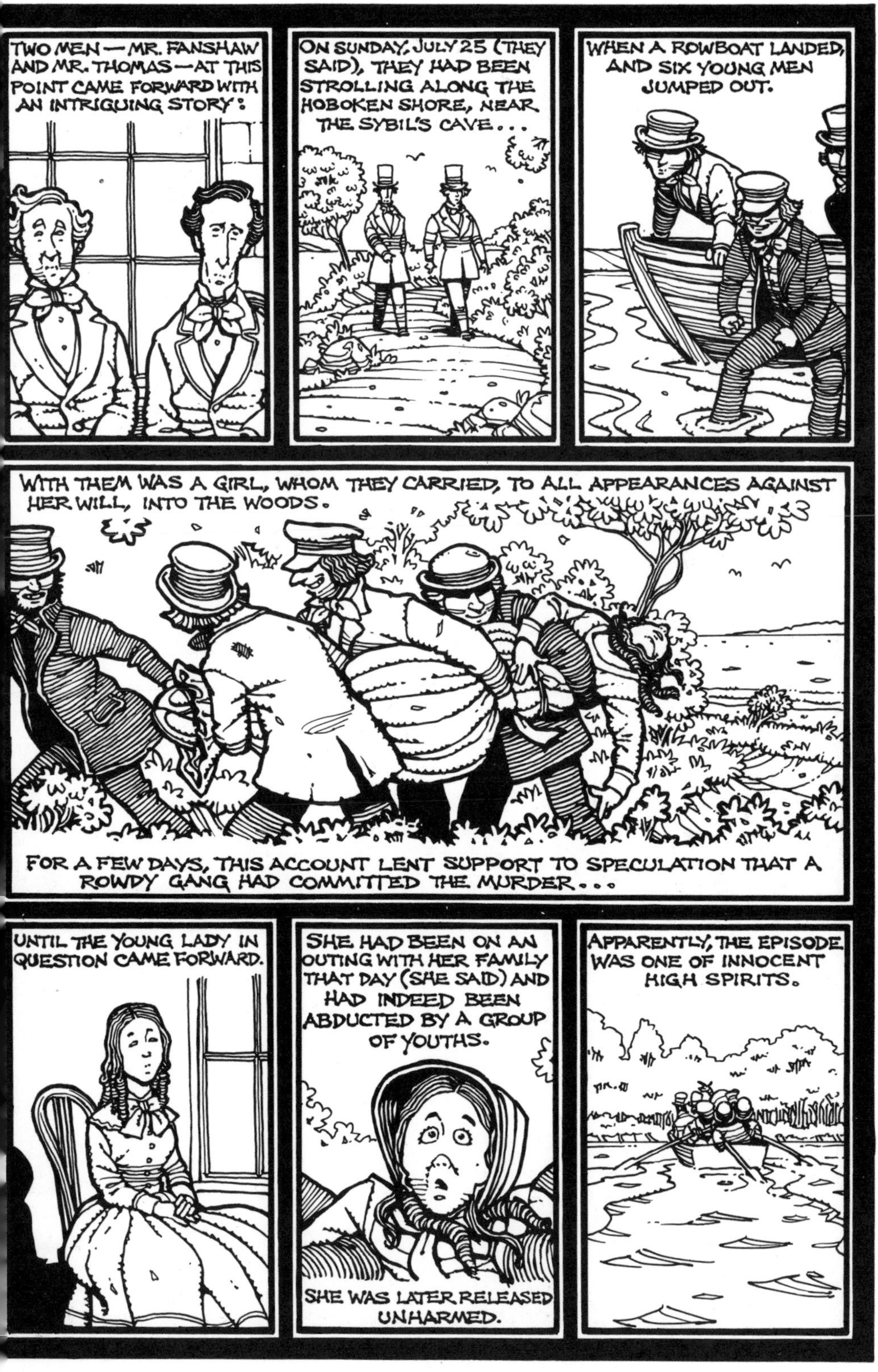
TWO MEN — MR. FANSHAW AND MR. THOMAS — AT THIS POINT CAME FORWARD WITH AN INTRIGUING STORY:
ON SUNDAY, JULY 25 (THEY SAID), THEY HAD BEEN STROLLING ALONG THE HOBOKEN SHORE, NEAR THE SYBIL'S CAVE...
WHEN A ROWBOAT LANDED, AND SIX YOUNG MEN JUMPED OUT.
WITH THEM WAS A GIRL, WHOM THEY CARRIED, TO ALL APPEARANCES AGAINST HER WILL, INTO THE WOODS.
FOR A FEW DAYS, THIS ACCOUNT LENT SUPPORT TO SPECULATION THAT A ROWDY GANG HAD COMMITTED THE MURDER...
UNTIL THE YOUNG LADY IN QUESTION CAME FORWARD.
SHE HAD BEEN ON AN OUTING WITH HER FAMILY THAT DAY (SHE SAID) AND HAD INDEED BEEN ABDUCTED BY A GROUP OF YOUTHS.
SHE WAS LATER RELEASED UNHARMED.
APPARENTLY, THE EPISODE WAS ONE OF INNOCENT HIGH SPIRITS.

ALSO AT THIS TIME, A YOUNG SAILOR NAMED WILLIAM KIEKUK WAS REMOVED FROM HIS SHIP, THE NORTH CAROLINA, AND PLACED UNDER ARREST.

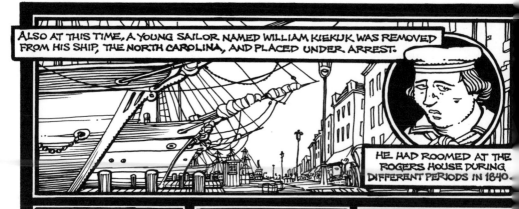

HE HAD ROOMED AT THE ROGERS HOUSE DURING DIFFERENT PERIODS IN 1840.

AND HAD BEEN OBSERVED BOARDING THE SHIP ON THE NIGHT OF SUNDAY, JULY 25, LATE AND IN A GREAT HURRY.

IN ADDITION, DARK STAINS COULD BE SEEN IN PLACES ON HIS TROUSERS.

(THESE TURNED OUT TO BE QUITE INNOCENT.)

KIEKUK ADMITTED HAVING KNOWN MARY, BUT HAD NOT BEEN ONE OF HER SUITORS.

HE HAD LAST SEEN HER, HE SAID, ON JULY 3.

IN ANY CASE, HE HAD SPENT THE SUNDAY IN QUESTION IN THE COMPANY OF FRIENDS AND RELATIONS WHO COULD AMPLY ACCOUNT FOR HIS MOVEMENTS.

NEVERTHELESS, HE REMAINED UNDER SUSPICION

NORTH CAROLI

AND WAS REMOVED FROM HIS SHIP THREE MORE TIMES OVER THE ENSUING WEEKS FOR FURTHER INTERROGATION.

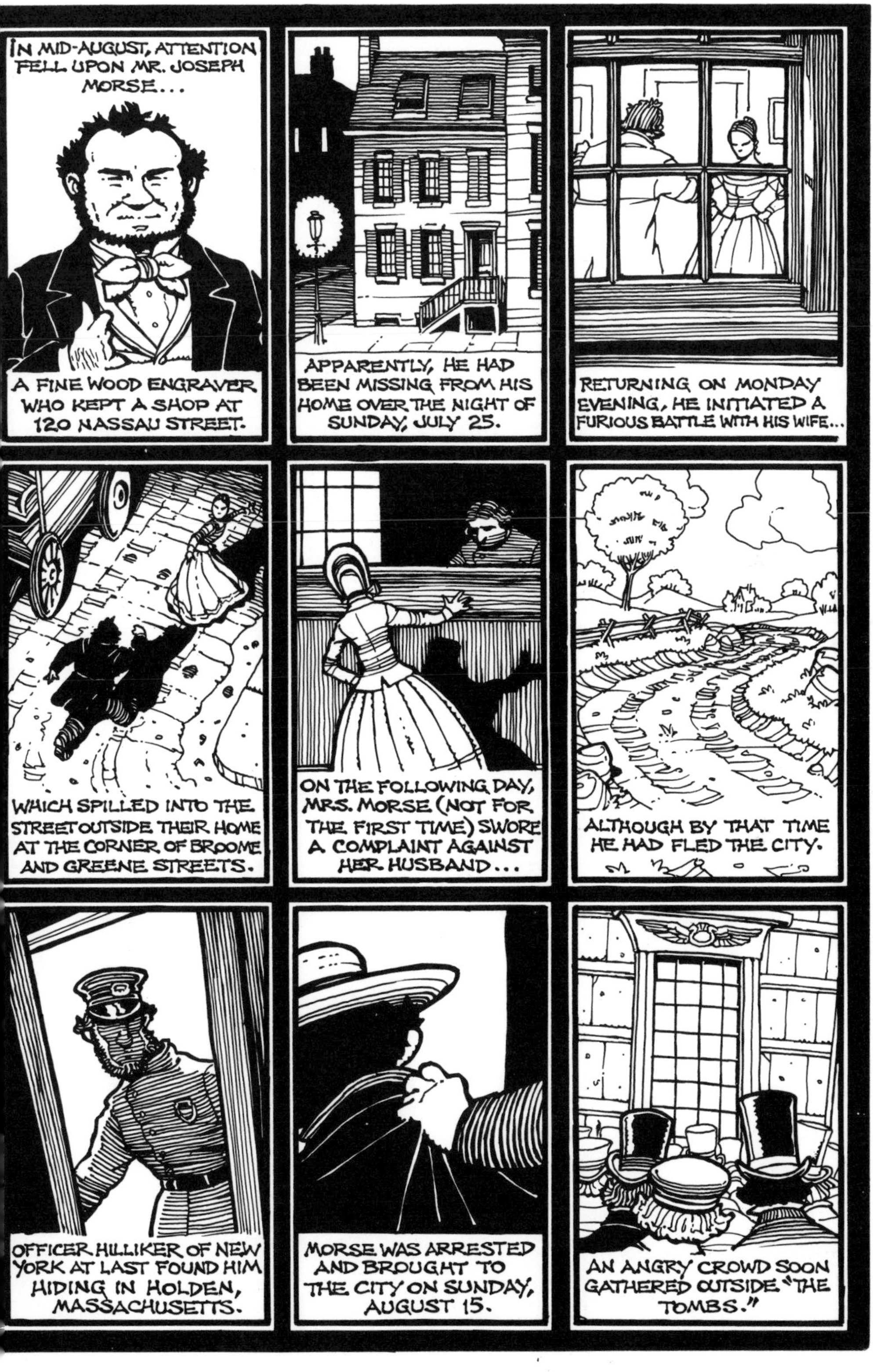
IN MID-AUGUST, ATTENTION FELL UPON MR. JOSEPH MORSE...
A FINE WOOD ENGRAVER WHO KEPT A SHOP AT 120 NASSAU STREET.
APPARENTLY, HE HAD BEEN MISSING FROM HIS HOME OVER THE NIGHT OF SUNDAY, JULY 25.
RETURNING ON MONDAY EVENING, HE INITIATED A FURIOUS BATTLE WITH HIS WIFE...
WHICH SPILLED INTO THE STREET OUTSIDE THEIR HOME AT THE CORNER OF BROOME AND GREENE STREETS.
ON THE FOLLOWING DAY, MRS. MORSE (NOT FOR THE FIRST TIME) SWORE A COMPLAINT AGAINST HER HUSBAND...
ALTHOUGH BY THAT TIME HE HAD FLED THE CITY.
OFFICER HILLIKER OF NEW YORK AT LAST FOUND HIM HIDING IN HOLDEN, MASSACHUSETTS.
MORSE WAS ARRESTED AND BROUGHT TO THE CITY ON SUNDAY, AUGUST 15.
AN ANGRY CROWD SOON GATHERED OUTSIDE "THE TOMBS."

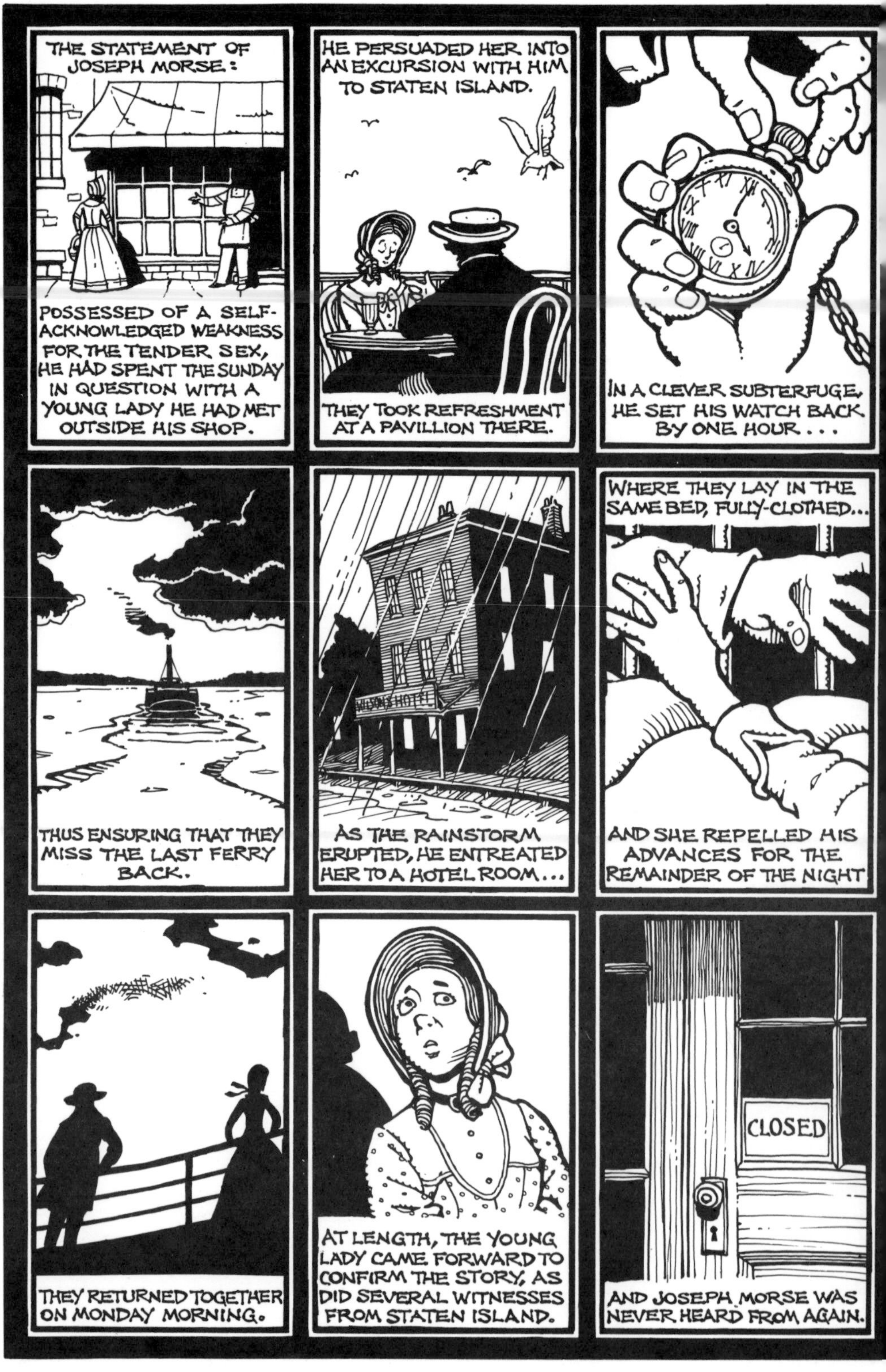
THE STATEMENT OF JOSEPH MORSE:
POSSESSED OF A SELF-ACKNOWLEDGED WEAKNESS FOR THE TENDER SEX, HE HAD SPENT THE SUNDAY IN QUESTION WITH A YOUNG LADY HE HAD MET OUTSIDE HIS SHOP.
HE PERSUADED HER INTO AN EXCURSION WITH HIM TO STATEN ISLAND.
THEY TOOK REFRESHMENT AT A PAVILLION THERE.
IN A CLEVER SUBTERFUGE, HE SET HIS WATCH BACK BY ONE HOUR...
THUS ENSURING THAT THEY MISS THE LAST FERRY BACK.
WILSON'S HOTEL
AS THE RAINSTORM ERUPTED, HE ENTREATED HER TO A HOTEL ROOM...
WHERE THEY LAY IN THE SAME BED, FULLY-CLOTHED...
AND SHE REPELLED HIS ADVANCES FOR THE REMAINDER OF THE NIGHT.
THEY RETURNED TOGETHER ON MONDAY MORNING.
AT LENGTH, THE YOUNG LADY CAME FORWARD TO CONFIRM THE STORY, AS DID SEVERAL WITNESSES FROM STATEN ISLAND.
CLOSED
AND JOSEPH MORSE WAS NEVER HEARD FROM AGAIN.

FRIDAY, AUGUST 27

THE UNFORTUNATE ARCHIBALD PADLEY WAS PLACED UNDER ARREST...

AND HELD IN "THE TOMBS" FOR THREE ENTIRE DAYS OF QUESTIONING.

HE INSISTED THAT HE WAS NEVER A SUITOR OF MARY'S AND HAD NO KNOWLEDGE OF HER ASSOCIATES.

VICTIM OF ILL-LUCK AND CIRCUMSTANCE, PADLEY WAS AT LAST RELEASED.

YET HE REMAINED UNDER SUSPICION—AS DID EVERY MAN KNOWN TO HAVE COME INTO CONTACT WITH THE DECEASED YOUNG LADY.

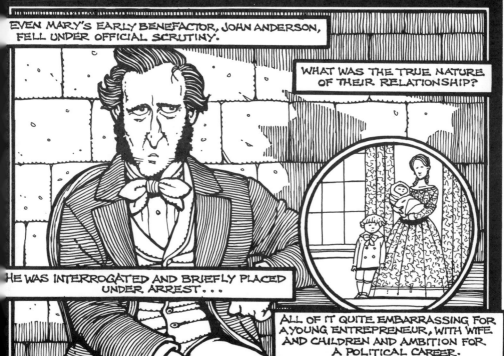

EVEN MARY'S EARLY BENEFACTOR, JOHN ANDERSON, FELL UNDER OFFICIAL SCRUTINY.

WHAT WAS THE TRUE NATURE OF THEIR RELATIONSHIP?

HE WAS INTERROGATED AND BRIEFLY PLACED UNDER ARREST...

ALL OF IT QUITE EMBARRASSING FOR A YOUNG ENTREPRENEUR, WITH WIFE AND CHILDREN AND AMBITION FOR A POLITICAL CAREER.

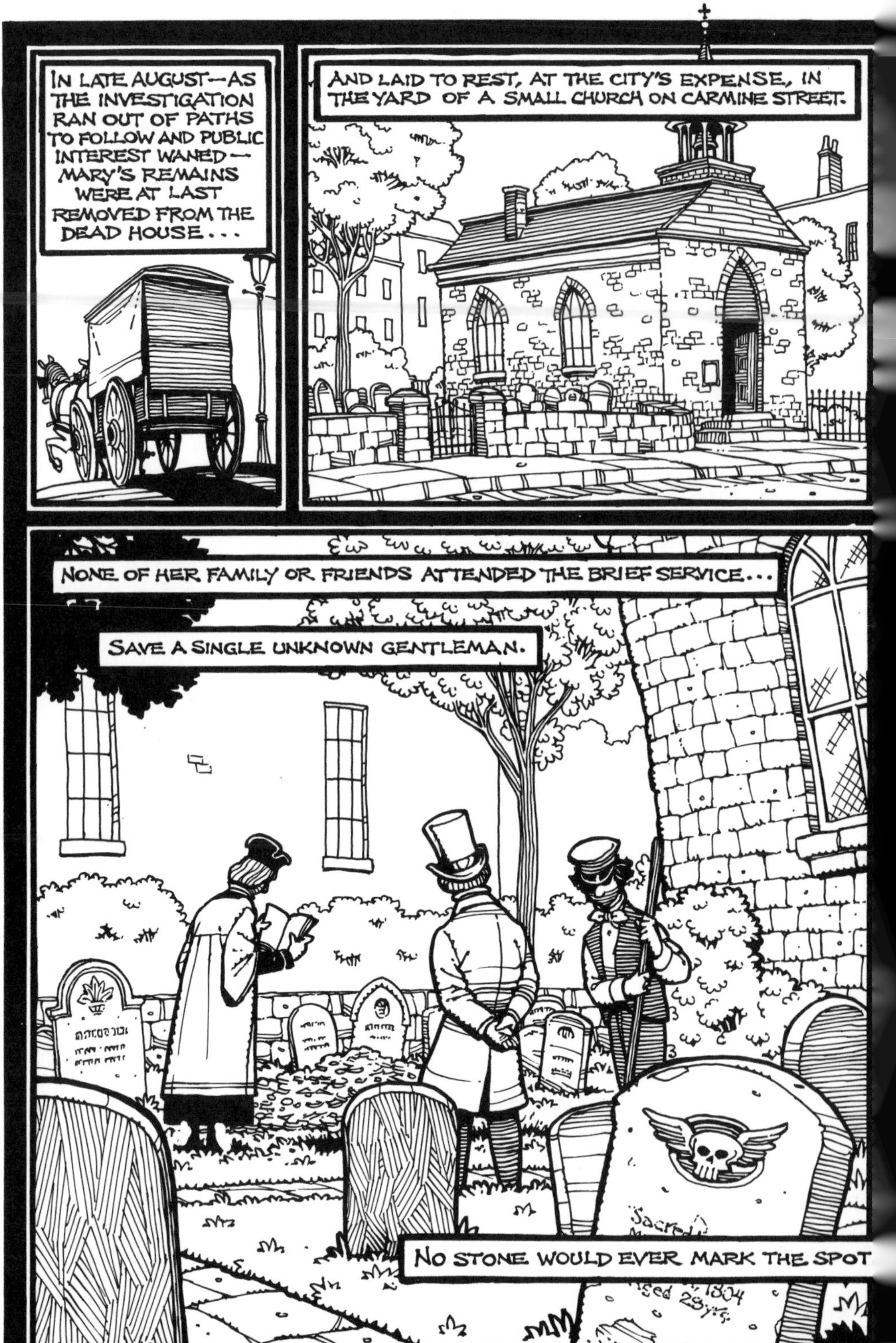

IN LATE AUGUST—AS THE INVESTIGATION RAN OUT OF PATHS TO FOLLOW AND PUBLIC INTEREST WANED—MARY'S REMAINS WERE AT LAST REMOVED FROM THE DEAD HOUSE . . .
AND LAID TO REST, AT THE CITY'S EXPENSE, IN THE YARD OF A SMALL CHURCH ON CARMINE STREET.
NONE OF HER FAMILY OR FRIENDS ATTENDED THE BRIEF SERVICE . . .
SAVE A SINGLE UNKNOWN GENTLEMAN.
NO STONE WOULD EVER MARK THE SPOT

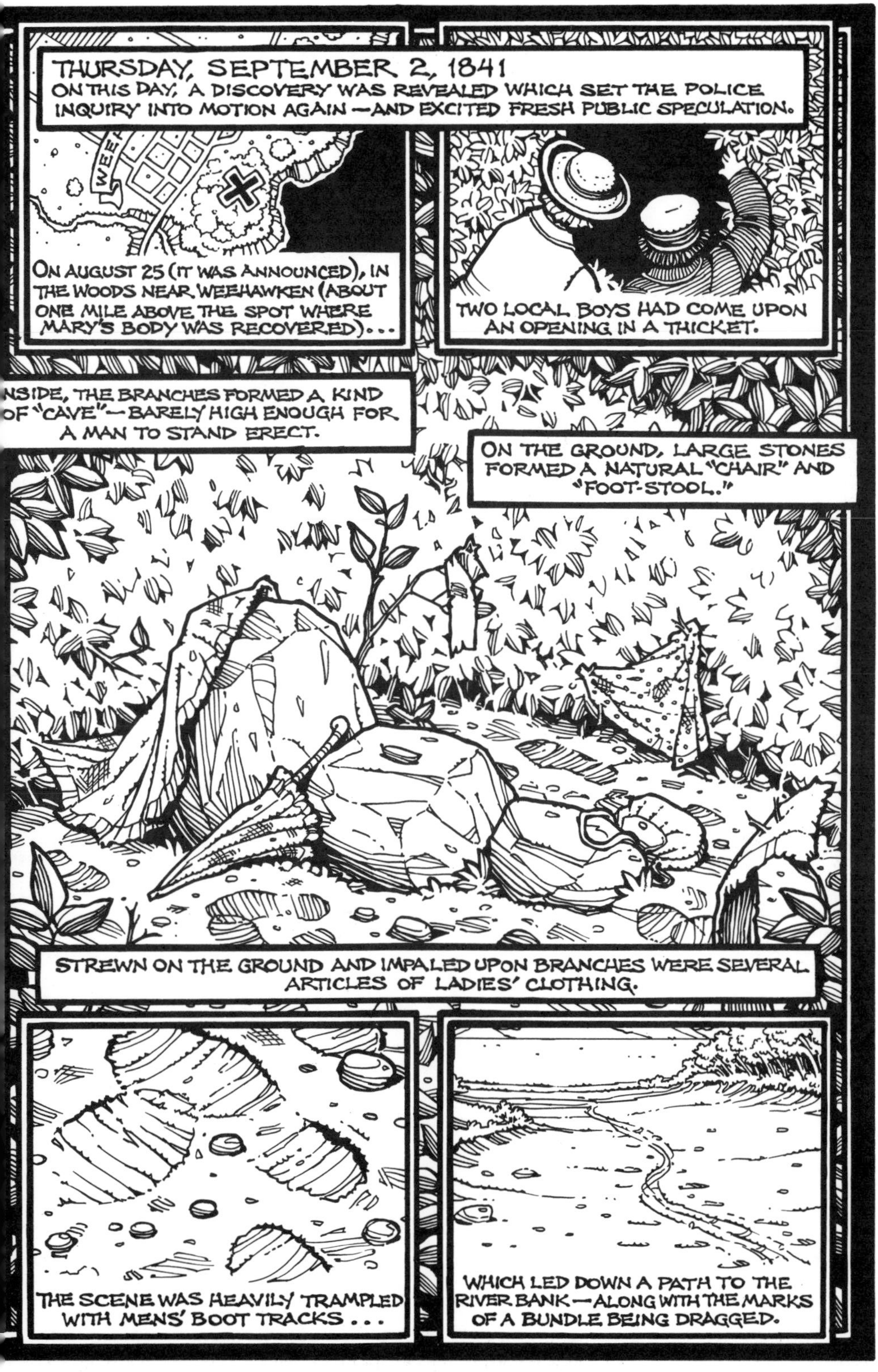
THURSDAY, SEPTEMBER 2, 1841
ON THIS DAY, A DISCOVERY WAS REVEALED WHICH SET THE POLICE INQUIRY INTO MOTION AGAIN — AND EXCITED FRESH PUBLIC SPECULATION.
WEE
ON AUGUST 25 (IT WAS ANNOUNCED), IN THE WOODS NEAR WEEHAWKEN (ABOUT ONE MILE ABOVE THE SPOT WHERE MARY'S BODY WAS RECOVERED)...
TWO LOCAL BOYS HAD COME UPON AN OPENING IN A THICKET.
INSIDE, THE BRANCHES FORMED A KIND OF "CAVE" — BARELY HIGH ENOUGH FOR A MAN TO STAND ERECT.
ON THE GROUND, LARGE STONES FORMED A NATURAL "CHAIR" AND "FOOT-STOOL."
STREWN ON THE GROUND AND IMPALED UPON BRANCHES WERE SEVERAL ARTICLES OF LADIES' CLOTHING.
THE SCENE WAS HEAVILY TRAMPLED WITH MENS' BOOT TRACKS ...
WHICH LED DOWN A PATH TO THE RIVER BANK — ALONG WITH THE MARKS OF A BUNDLE BEING DRAGGED.

THE TWO BOYS, CHARLES KELLENBARACK, AGE 16...

AND HIS BROTHER OSSIAN, AGE 12...

WERE THE YOUNGER SONS OF MRS. FREDERICA LOSS, A GERMAN WIDOW...

MOORE'S HOUSE

WHO OWNED AND OPERATED A NEARBY TAVERN CALLED NICK MOORE'S HOUSE...

A POPULAR STOPPING-SPOT FOR THOSE TAKING THE AIR ALONG THE SHORES OF THE HUDSON.

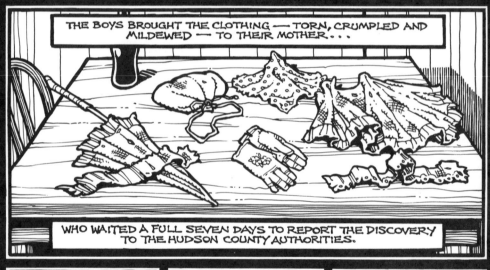

THE BOYS BROUGHT THE CLOTHING — TORN, CRUMPLED AND MILDEWED — TO THEIR MOTHER...

WHO WAITED A FULL SEVEN DAYS TO REPORT THE DISCOVERY TO THE HUDSON COUNTY AUTHORITIES.

IN DUE COURSE, MRS. ROGERS IDENTIFIED THE ARTICLES AS HAVING BELONGED TO HER DAUGHTER...

AND THE AREA AROUND WEEHAWKEN SWARMED WITH POLICE AND JOURNALISTS.

MRS. LOSS HAD A STORY READY FOR THEM.

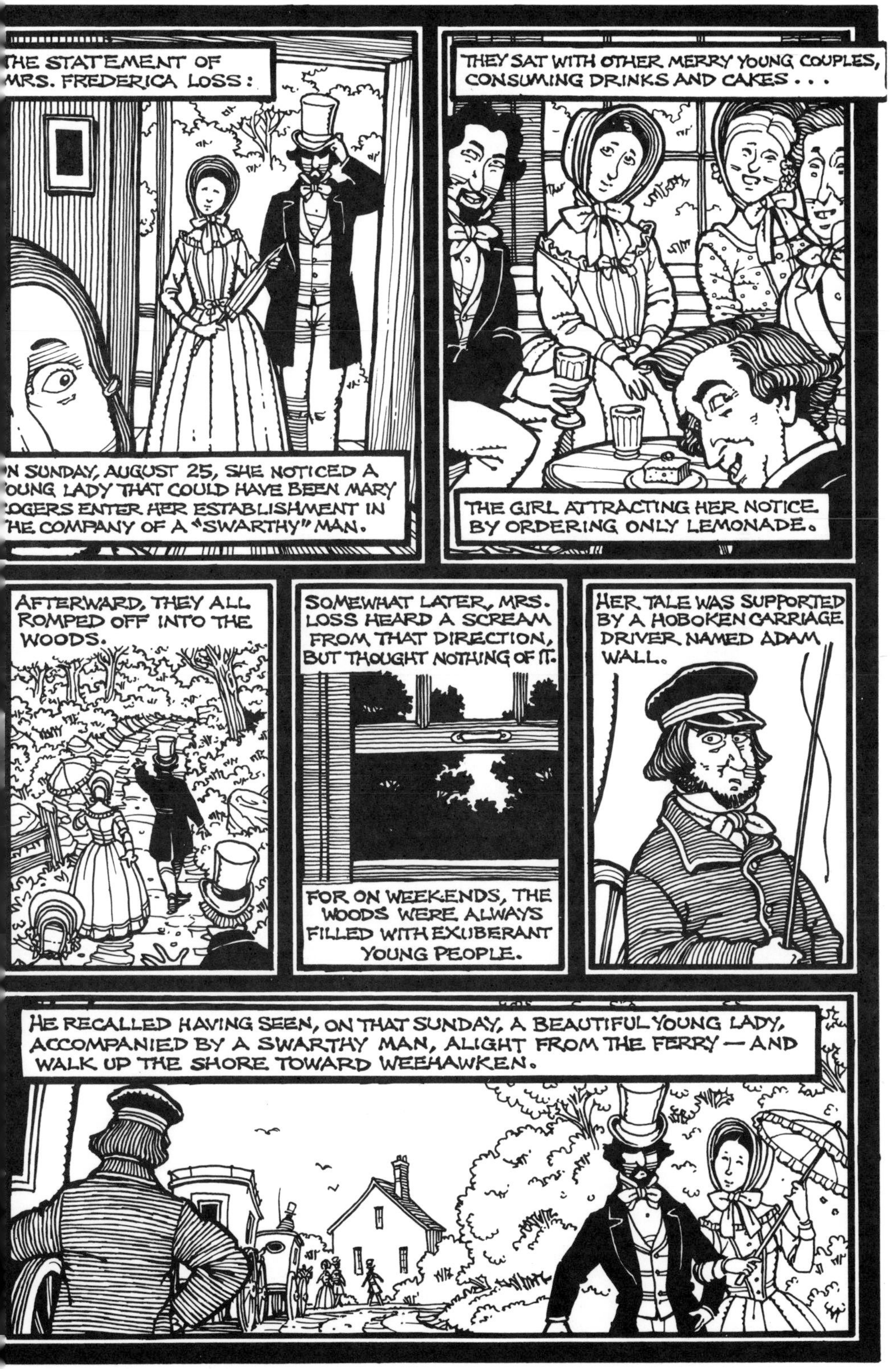
THE STATEMENT OF MRS. FREDERICA LOSS:
N SUNDAY, AUGUST 25, SHE NOTICED A OUNG LADY THAT COULD HAVE BEEN MARY OGERS ENTER HER ESTABLISHMENT IN HE COMPANY OF A "SWARTHY" MAN.
THEY SAT WITH OTHER MERRY YOUNG COUPLES, CONSUMING DRINKS AND CAKES . . .
THE GIRL ATTRACTING HER NOTICE BY ORDERING ONLY LEMONADE.
AFTERWARD, THEY ALL ROMPED OFF INTO THE WOODS.
SOMEWHAT LATER, MRS. LOSS HEARD A SCREAM FROM THAT DIRECTION, BUT THOUGHT NOTHING OF IT.
FOR ON WEEKENDS, THE WOODS WERE ALWAYS FILLED WITH EXUBERANT YOUNG PEOPLE.
HER TALE WAS SUPPORTED BY A HOBOKEN CARRIAGE DRIVER NAMED ADAM WALL.
HE RECALLED HAVING SEEN, ON THAT SUNDAY, A BEAUTIFUL YOUNG LADY, ACCOMPANIED BY A SWARTHY MAN, ALIGHT FROM THE FERRY — AND WALK UP THE SHORE TOWARD WEEHAWKEN.

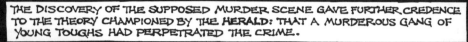

THE DISCOVERY OF THE SUPPOSED MURDER SCENE GAVE FURTHER CREDENCE TO THE THEORY CHAMPIONED BY THE *HERALD*: THAT A MURDEROUS GANG OF YOUNG TOUGHS HAD PERPETRATED THE CRIME.

IT WAS A KNOWN FACT THAT ON THAT PARTICULAR WEEKEND, TWO BOAT-LOADS OF RUFFIANS HAD COME OVER FROM MANHATTAN...

TO DRINK AND ROISTER AT A CERTAIN "RUM-HOLE" ON THE SHORE...

AFTER WHICH THEY ROAMED THE AREA WITH CLUBS AND KNIVES...

TERRORIZING INNOCENT YOUNG COUPLES.

IF MARY HAD BEEN ACCOMPANIED BY A MAN — SO THE THEORY WENT — HE WAS MOST LIKELY ALSO MURDERED BY THESE THUGS.

(NO CORRESPONDING MALE BODY, HOWEVER, WAS EVER RECOVERED.)

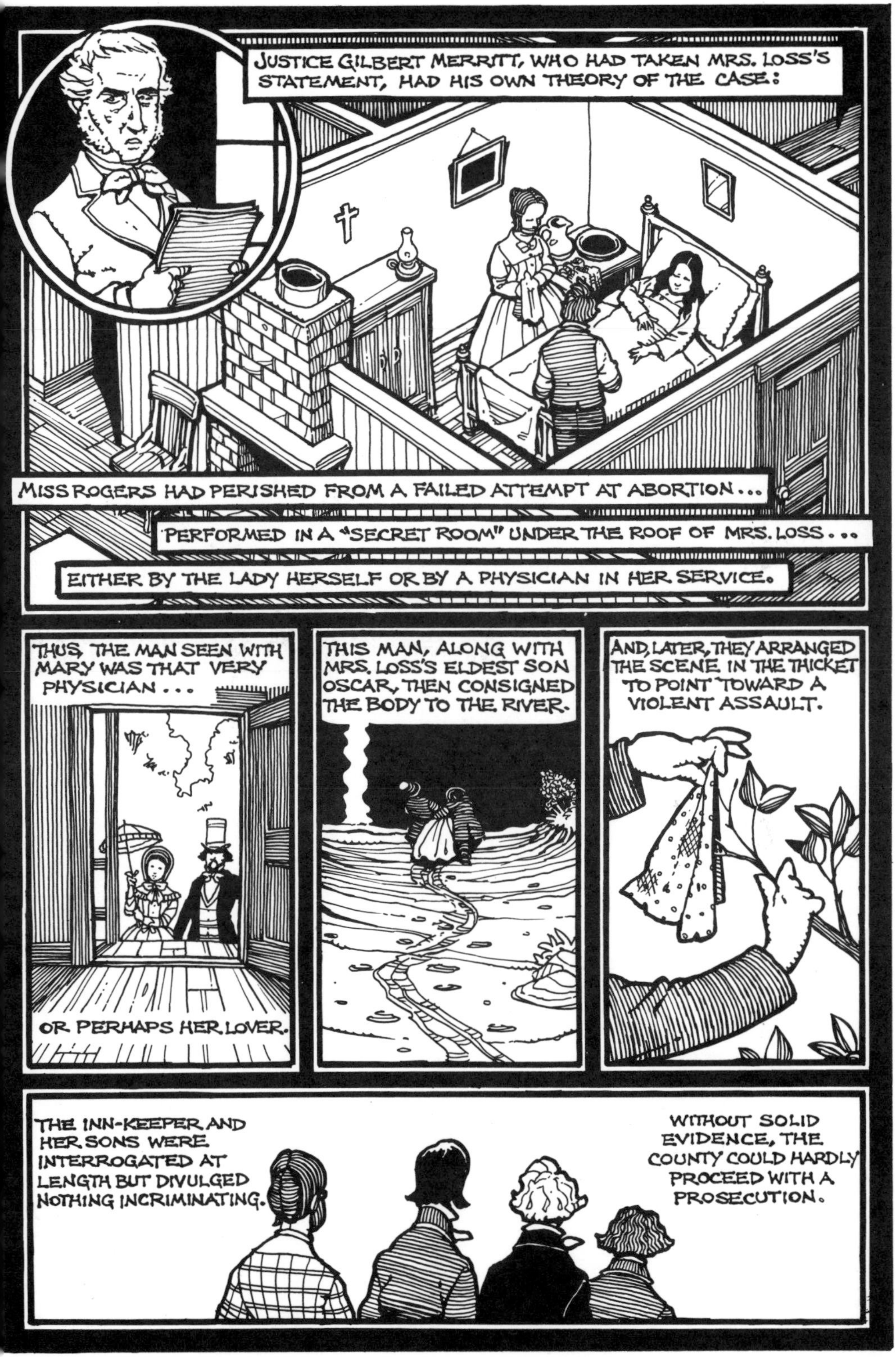
JUSTICE GILBERT MERRITT, WHO HAD TAKEN MRS. LOSS'S STATEMENT, HAD HIS OWN THEORY OF THE CASE:
MISS ROGERS HAD PERISHED FROM A FAILED ATTEMPT AT ABORTION...
PERFORMED IN A "SECRET ROOM" UNDER THE ROOF OF MRS. LOSS...
EITHER BY THE LADY HERSELF OR BY A PHYSICIAN IN HER SERVICE.
THUS, THE MAN SEEN WITH MARY WAS THAT VERY PHYSICIAN...
OR PERHAPS HER LOVER.
THIS MAN, ALONG WITH MRS. LOSS'S ELDEST SON OSCAR, THEN CONSIGNED THE BODY TO THE RIVER.
AND, LATER, THEY ARRANGED THE SCENE IN THE THICKET TO POINT TOWARD A VIOLENT ASSAULT.
THE INN-KEEPER AND HER SONS WERE INTERROGATED AT LENGTH BUT DIVULGED NOTHING INCRIMINATING.
WITHOUT SOLID EVIDENCE, THE COUNTY COULD HARDLY PROCEED WITH A PROSECUTION.

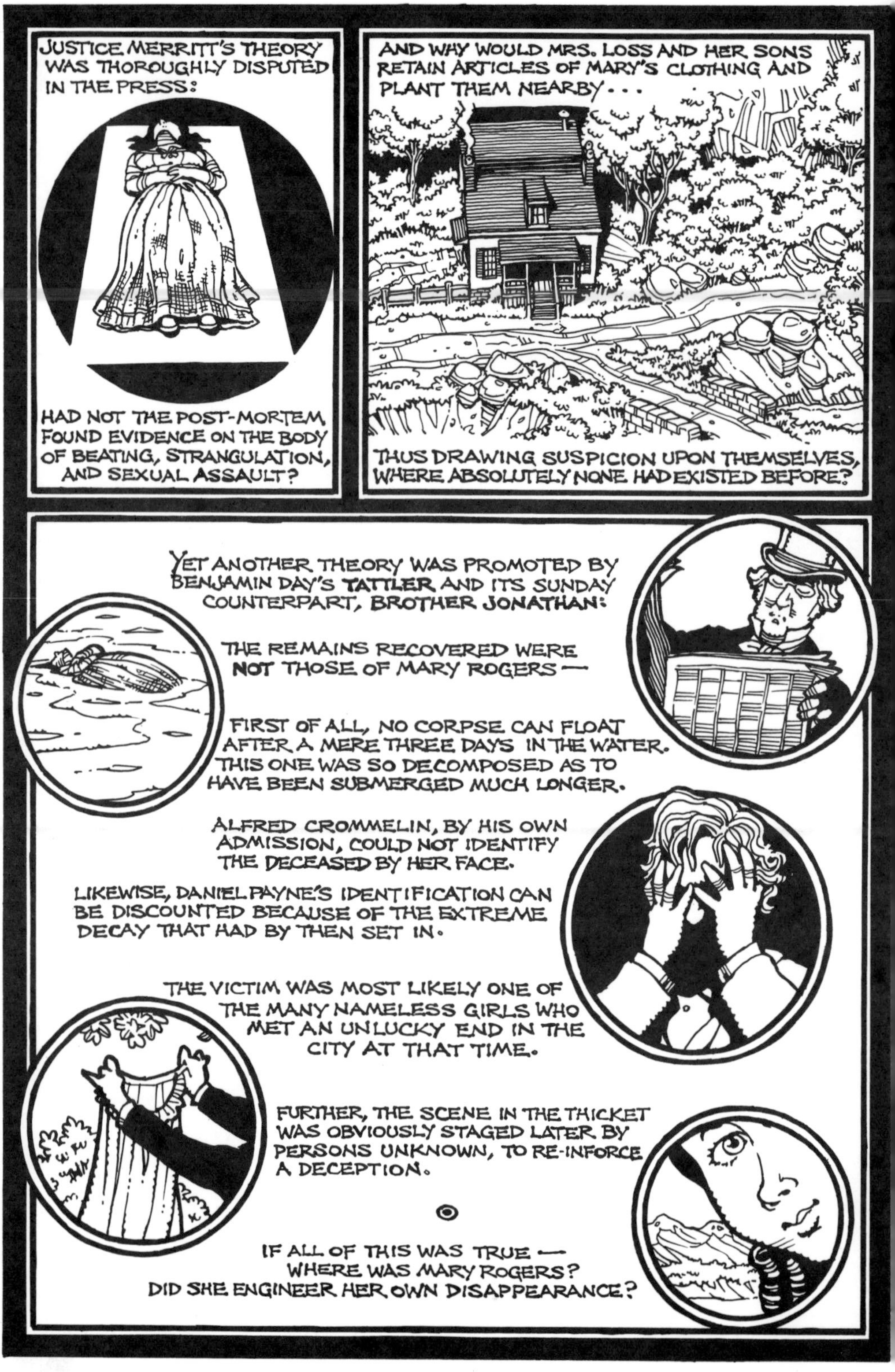

JUSTICE MERRITT'S THEORY WAS THOROUGHLY DISPUTED IN THE PRESS:
HAD NOT THE POST-MORTEM FOUND EVIDENCE ON THE BODY OF BEATING, STRANGULATION, AND SEXUAL ASSAULT?
AND WHY WOULD MRS. LOSS AND HER SONS RETAIN ARTICLES OF MARY'S CLOTHING AND PLANT THEM NEARBY . . .
THUS DRAWING SUSPICION UPON THEMSELVES, WHERE ABSOLUTELY NONE HAD EXISTED BEFORE?
YET ANOTHER THEORY WAS PROMOTED BY BENJAMIN DAY'S TATTLER AND ITS SUNDAY COUNTERPART, BROTHER JONATHAN:
THE REMAINS RECOVERED WERE NOT THOSE OF MARY ROGERS —
FIRST OF ALL, NO CORPSE CAN FLOAT AFTER A MERE THREE DAYS IN THE WATER. THIS ONE WAS SO DECOMPOSED AS TO HAVE BEEN SUBMERGED MUCH LONGER.
ALFRED CROMMELIN, BY HIS OWN ADMISSION, COULD NOT IDENTIFY THE DECEASED BY HER FACE.
LIKEWISE, DANIEL PAYNE'S IDENTIFICATION CAN BE DISCOUNTED BECAUSE OF THE EXTREME DECAY THAT HAD BY THEN SET IN.
THE VICTIM WAS MOST LIKELY ONE OF THE MANY NAMELESS GIRLS WHO MET AN UNLUCKY END IN THE CITY AT THAT TIME.
FURTHER, THE SCENE IN THE THICKET WAS OBVIOUSLY STAGED LATER BY PERSONS UNKNOWN, TO RE-INFORCE A DECEPTION.
IF ALL OF THIS WAS TRUE — WHERE WAS MARY ROGERS? DID SHE ENGINEER HER OWN DISAPPEARANCE?

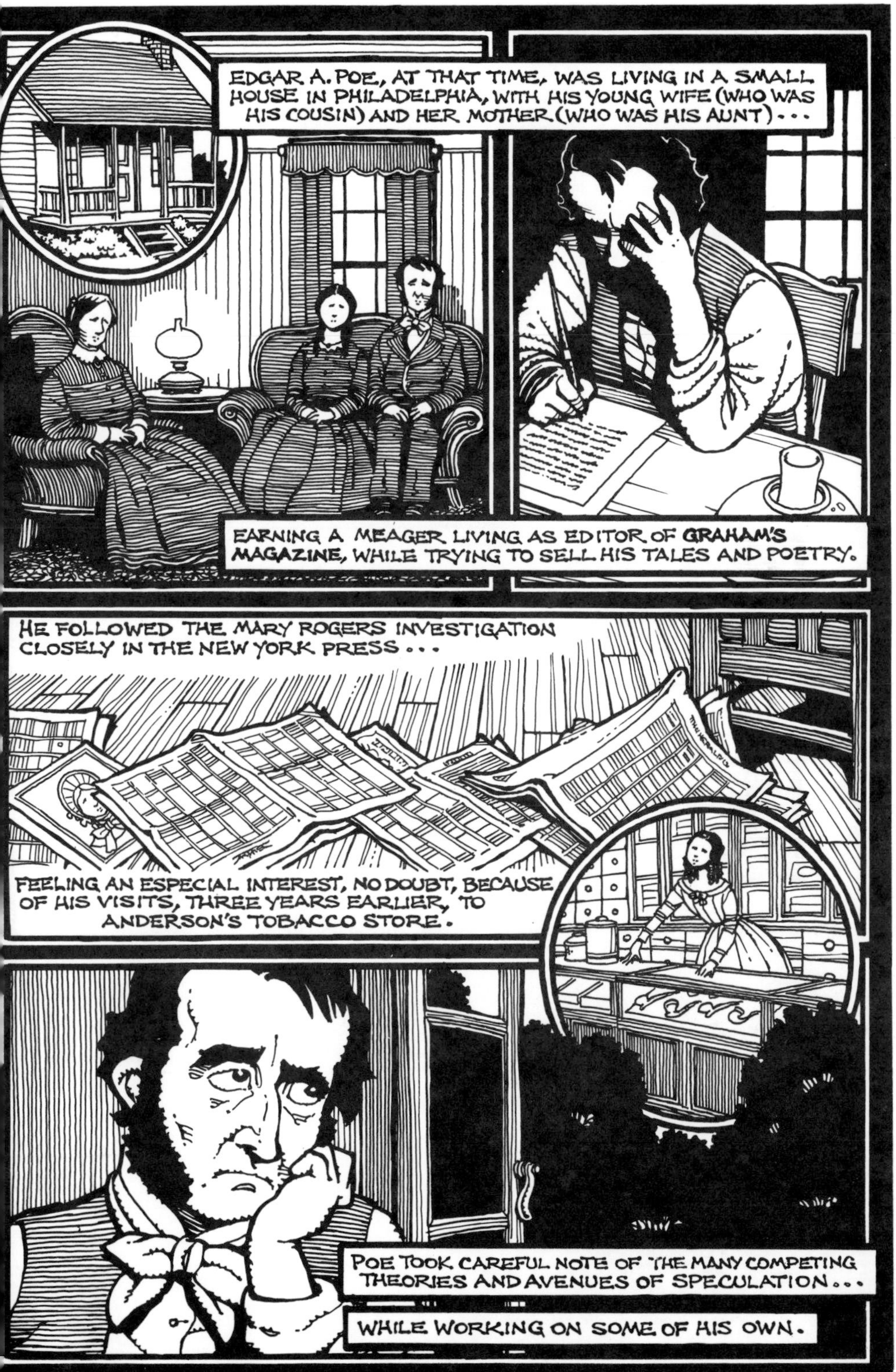
EDGAR A. POE, AT THAT TIME, WAS LIVING IN A SMALL HOUSE IN PHILADELPHIA, WITH HIS YOUNG WIFE (WHO WAS HIS COUSIN) AND HER MOTHER (WHO WAS HIS AUNT)...
EARNING A MEAGER LIVING AS EDITOR OF GRAHAM'S MAGAZINE, WHILE TRYING TO SELL HIS TALES AND POETRY.
HE FOLLOWED THE MARY ROGERS INVESTIGATION CLOSELY IN THE NEW YORK PRESS...
FEELING AN ESPECIAL INTEREST, NO DOUBT, BECAUSE OF HIS VISITS, THREE YEARS EARLIER, TO ANDERSON'S TOBACCO STORE.
POE TOOK CAREFUL NOTE OF THE MANY COMPETING THEORIES AND AVENUES OF SPECULATION...
WHILE WORKING ON SOME OF HIS OWN.

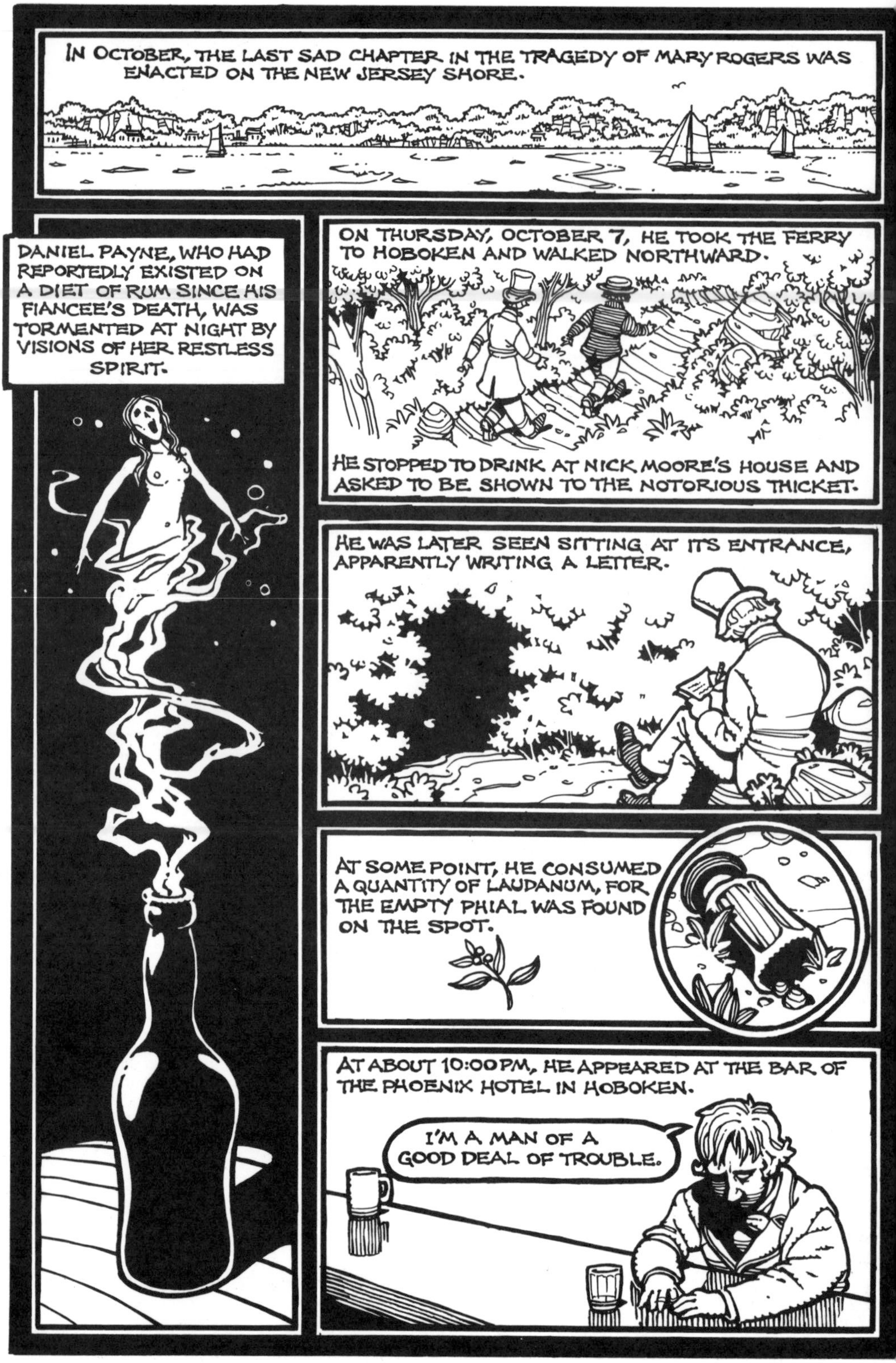
IN OCTOBER, THE LAST SAD CHAPTER IN THE TRAGEDY OF MARY ROGERS WAS ENACTED ON THE NEW JERSEY SHORE.
DANIEL PAYNE, WHO HAD REPORTEDLY EXISTED ON A DIET OF RUM SINCE HIS FIANCEE'S DEATH, WAS TORMENTED AT NIGHT BY VISIONS OF HER RESTLESS SPIRIT.
ON THURSDAY, OCTOBER 7, HE TOOK THE FERRY TO HOBOKEN AND WALKED NORTHWARD.
HE STOPPED TO DRINK AT NICK MOORE'S HOUSE AND ASKED TO BE SHOWN TO THE NOTORIOUS THICKET.
HE WAS LATER SEEN SITTING AT ITS ENTRANCE, APPARENTLY WRITING A LETTER.
AT SOME POINT, HE CONSUMED A QUANTITY OF LAUDANUM, FOR THE EMPTY PHIAL WAS FOUND ON THE SPOT.
AT ABOUT 10:00 PM, HE APPEARED AT THE BAR OF THE PHOENIX HOTEL IN HOBOKEN.
I'M A MAN OF A GOOD DEAL OF TROUBLE.

THE NEXT MORNING, PAYNE WAS SEEN LYING IN A PATCH OF WEEDS AT THE CENTER OF TOWN.

LATER, HE WANDERED THE WOODS BLINDLY, AS THE DRUG TOOK ITS DEADLY EFFECT.

AT LAST, HIS LIFELESS FORM WAS FOUND BESIDE THE PATH TO THE SIBYL'S CAVE, LOOKING OUT TOWARD THE RIVER.

AMONG THE PAPERS RECOVERED FROM HIS PERSON WAS A HAND-WRITTEN NOTE—

TO THE WORLD— HERE I AM ON THE VERY SPOT. MAY GOD FORGIVE ME FOR MY MISSPENT LIFE.

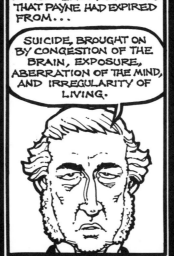
THE CORONER'S INQUEST, PRESIDED OVER BY JUSTICE MERRITT, CONCLUDED THAT PAYNE HAD EXPIRED FROM...

SUICIDE, BROUGHT ON BY CONGESTION OF THE BRAIN, EXPOSURE, ABERRATION OF THE MIND, AND IRREGULARITY OF LIVING.

THE OTHER PAPERS FOUND IN HIS POCKETS WERE HELD TO BE OF LITTLE INTEREST AND NOT RELEASED TO THE PUBLIC.

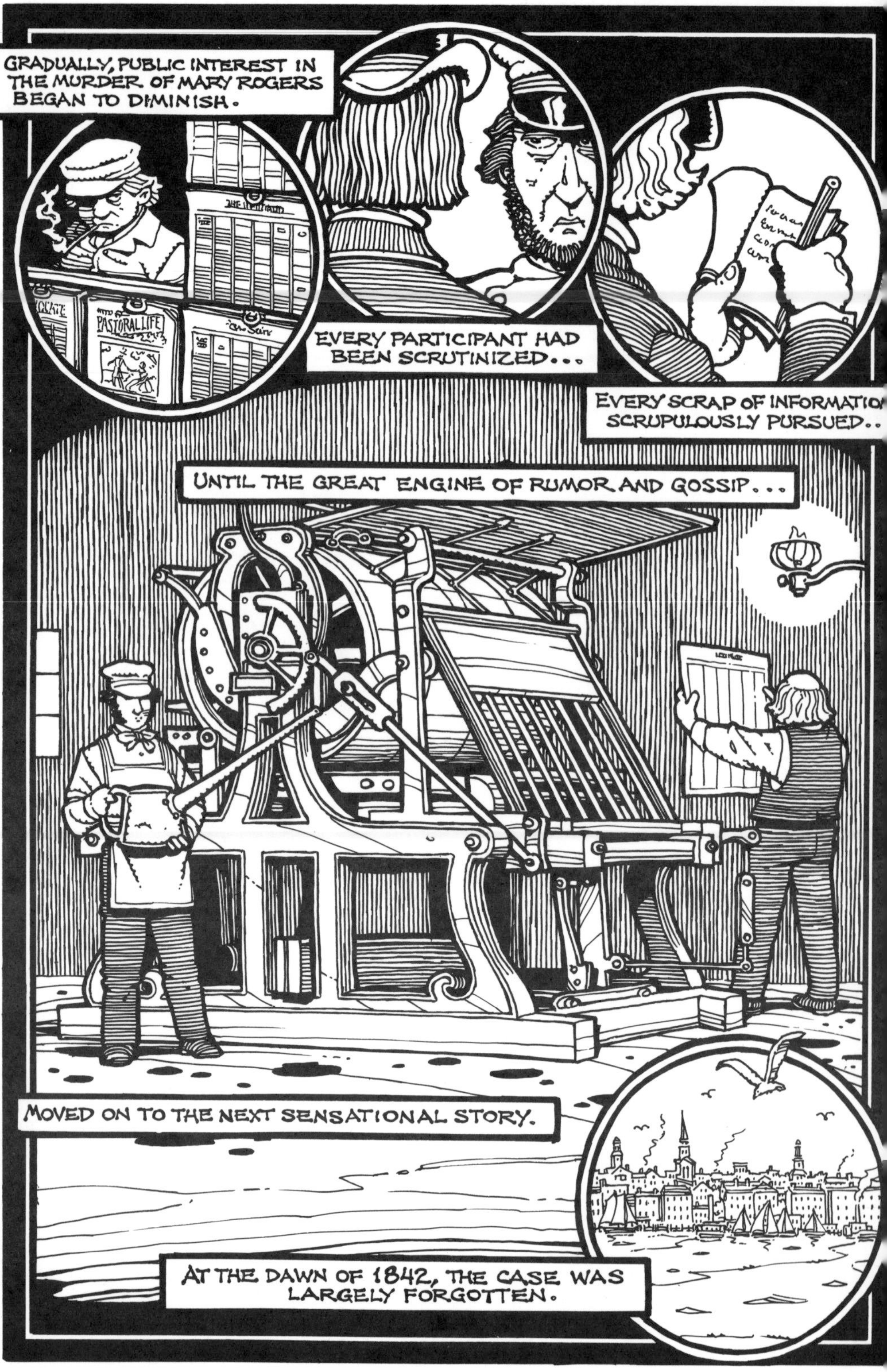
GRADUALLY, PUBLIC INTEREST IN THE MURDER OF MARY ROGERS BEGAN TO DIMINISH.
PASTORAL LIFE
EVERY PARTICIPANT HAD BEEN SCRUTINIZED...
EVERY SCRAP OF INFORMATIO
SCRUPULOUSLY PURSUED..
UNTIL THE GREAT ENGINE OF RUMOR AND GOSSIP...
MOVED ON TO THE NEXT SENSATIONAL STORY.
AT THE DAWN OF 1842, THE CASE WAS LARGELY FORGOTTEN.

PART IV.
EDGAR A. POE.

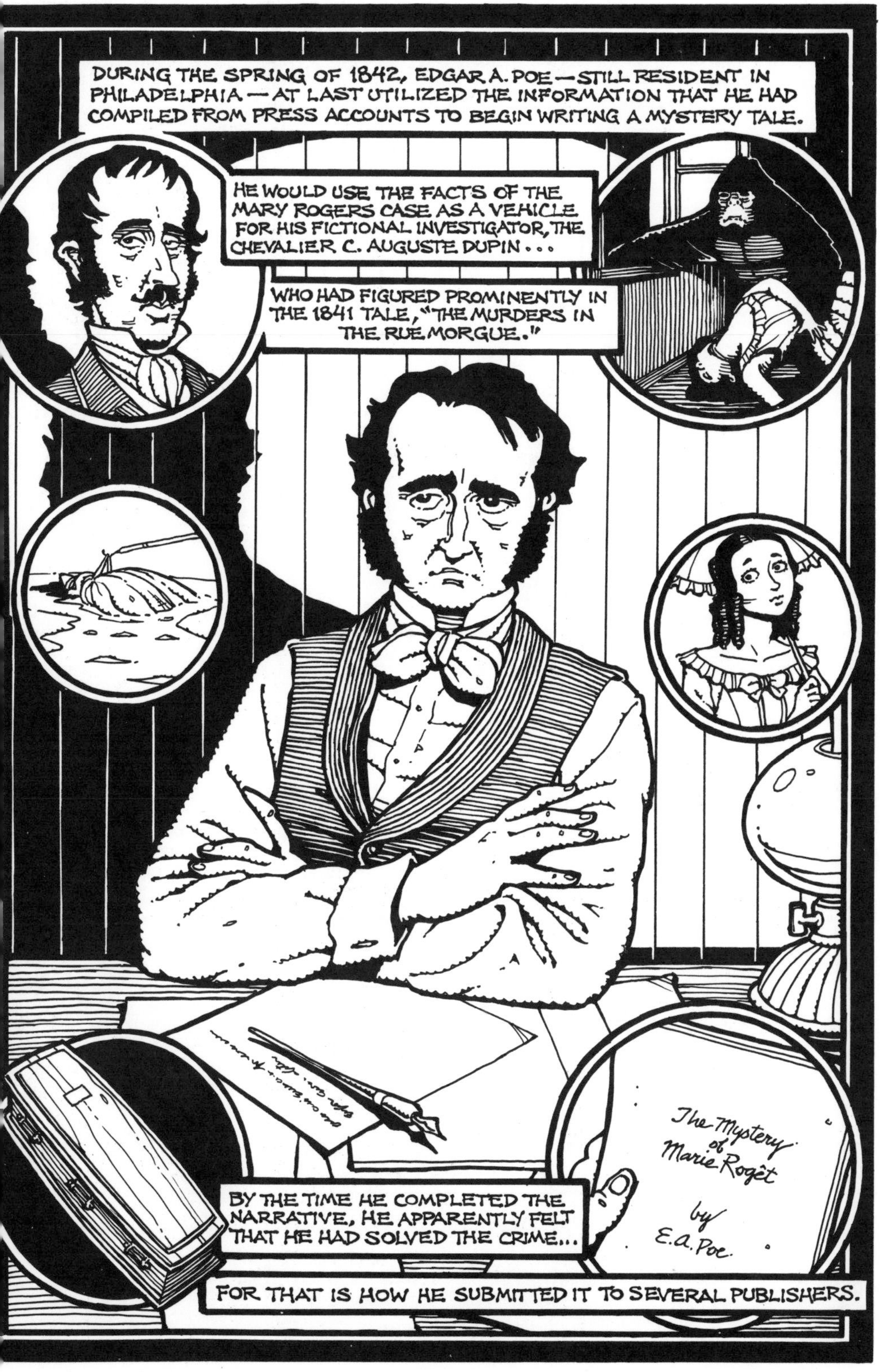
DURING THE SPRING OF 1842, EDGAR A. POE — STILL RESIDENT IN PHILADELPHIA — AT LAST UTILIZED THE INFORMATION THAT HE HAD COMPILED FROM PRESS ACCOUNTS TO BEGIN WRITING A MYSTERY TALE.
HE WOULD USE THE FACTS OF THE MARY ROGERS CASE AS A VEHICLE FOR HIS FICTIONAL INVESTIGATOR, THE CHEVALIER C. AUGUSTE DUPIN . . .
WHO HAD FIGURED PROMINENTLY IN THE 1841 TALE, "THE MURDERS IN THE RUE MORGUE."
The Mystery of Marie Rogêt by E.A. Poe
BY THE TIME HE COMPLETED THE NARRATIVE, HE APPARENTLY FELT THAT HE HAD SOLVED THE CRIME...
FOR THAT IS HOW HE SUBMITTED IT TO SEVERAL PUBLISHERS.

THE MYSTERY OF MARIE ROGÊT ALTHOUGH SET BY THE AUTHOR IN PARIS, THE CHARACTERS WERE EASY ENOUGH TO RECOGNIZE.

BEAUTIFUL MARIE IS THE DAUGHTER OF MME. ESTELLE ROGÊT...

WHO KEEPS A PENSION IN THE RUE PAVÉE SAINT ANDRÉE

SHE WORKS AT THE SHOP OF A PARFUMIER, M. LE BLANC...

WHERE SHE IS SURROUNDED BY ADMIRERS.

A PARTICULARLY ARDENT SUITOR IS THE GALLANT M. BEAUVAIS.

BUT MARIE BECOMES ENGAGED TO THE DISSIPATED M. EUSTACHE.

SHE LEAVES HOME ONE MORNING, TO VISIT AN AUNT IN THE RUE DES DRÔMES.

THREE DAYS LATER, HER CORPSE IS FOUND DRIFTING IN THE SEINE, BEATEN AND STRANGLED.

THE SO-CALLED MURDER SCENE IS DISCOVERED IN THE WOODS OF THE BARRIÈRE DU ROULE...

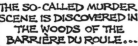

NEAR THE PUBLIC HOUSE OF MME. DULAC...

WHO CLAIMS TO HAVE SEEN THE VICTIM IN THE COMPANY OF A "SWARTHY MAN."

WITH ONLY NEWSPAPER ACCOUNTS TO GUIDE HIM, DUPIN TAKES ON THE MYSTERY.

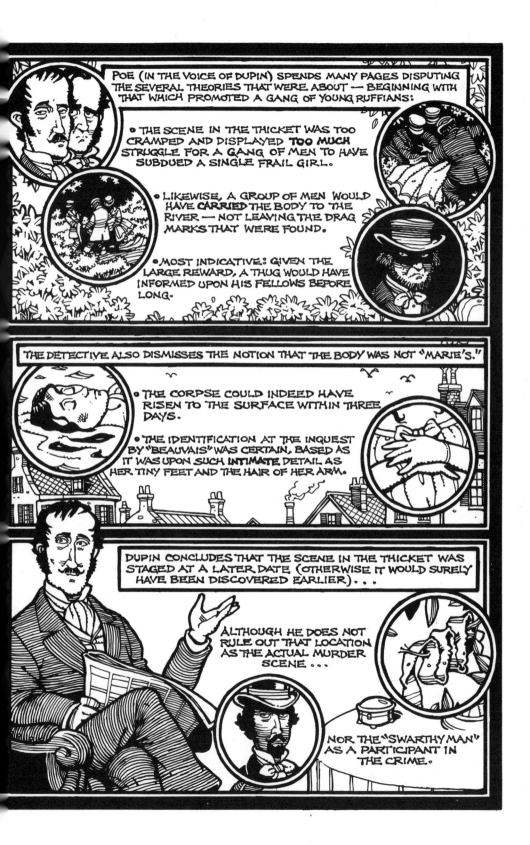

POE (IN THE VOICE OF DUPIN) SPENDS MANY PAGES DISPUTING THE SEVERAL THEORIES THAT WERE ABOUT — BEGINNING WITH THAT WHICH PROMOTED A GANG OF YOUNG RUFFIANS:

• THE SCENE IN THE THICKET WAS TOO CRAMPED AND DISPLAYED **TOO MUCH** STRUGGLE FOR A GANG OF MEN TO HAVE SUBDUED A SINGLE FRAIL GIRL.

• LIKEWISE, A GROUP OF MEN WOULD HAVE **CARRIED** THE BODY TO THE RIVER — NOT LEAVING THE DRAG MARKS THAT WERE FOUND.

• MOST INDICATIVE: GIVEN THE LARGE REWARD, A THUG WOULD HAVE INFORMED UPON HIS FELLOWS BEFORE LONG.

THE DETECTIVE ALSO DISMISSES THE NOTION THAT THE BODY WAS NOT "MARIE'S."

• THE CORPSE COULD INDEED HAVE RISEN TO THE SURFACE WITHIN THREE DAYS.

• THE IDENTIFICATION AT THE INQUEST BY "BEAUVAIS" WAS CERTAIN, BASED AS IT WAS UPON SUCH **INTIMATE** DETAIL AS HER TINY FEET AND THE HAIR OF HER ARM.

DUPIN CONCLUDES THAT THE SCENE IN THE THICKET WAS STAGED AT A LATER DATE (OTHERWISE IT WOULD SURELY HAVE BEEN DISCOVERED EARLIER)...

ALTHOUGH HE DOES NOT RULE OUT THAT LOCATION AS THE ACTUAL MURDER SCENE...

NOR THE "SWARTHY MAN" AS A PARTICIPANT IN THE CRIME.

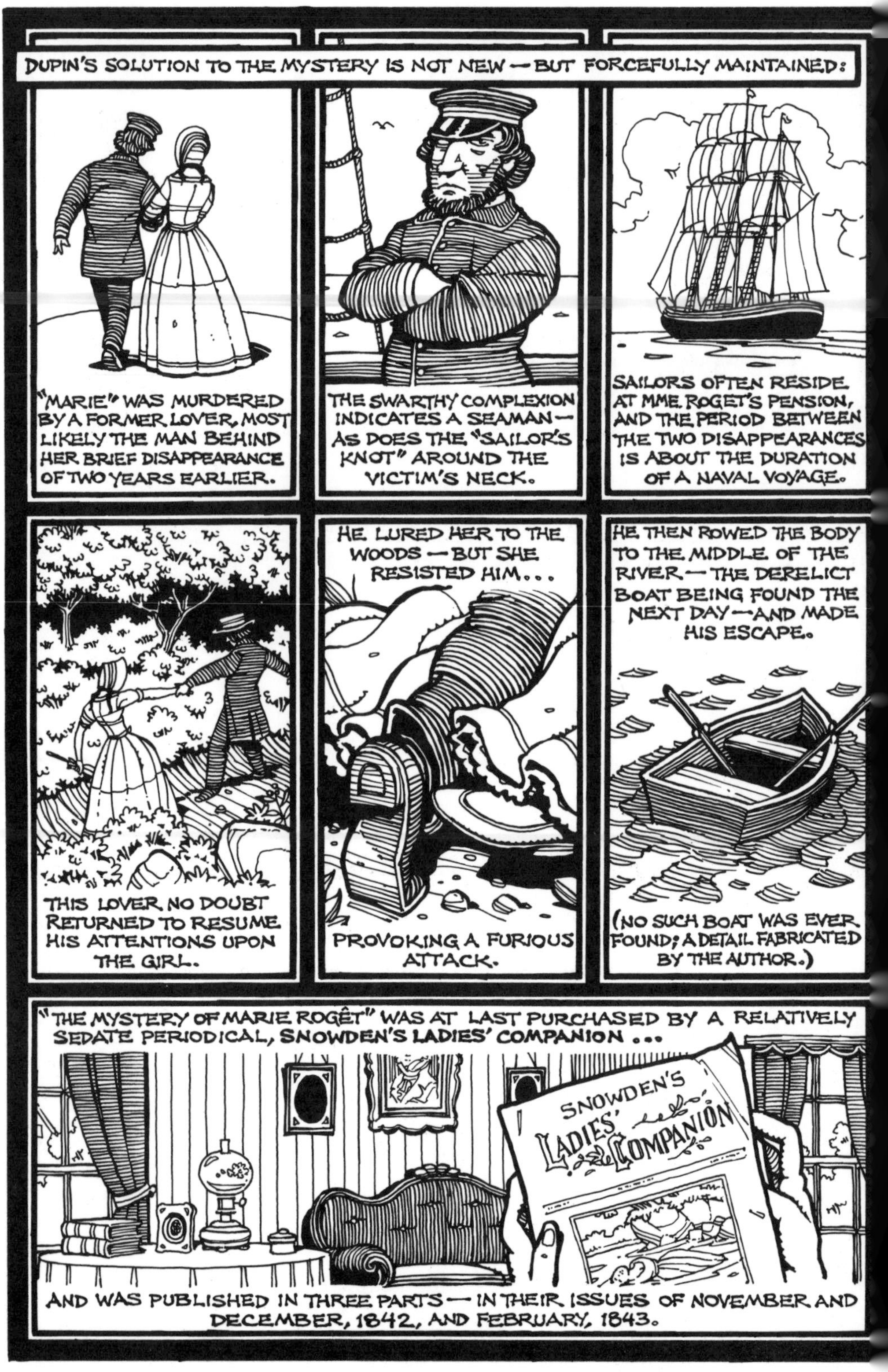
DUPIN'S SOLUTION TO THE MYSTERY IS NOT NEW — BUT FORCEFULLY MAINTAINED:
"MARIE" WAS MURDERED BY A FORMER LOVER, MOST LIKELY THE MAN BEHIND HER BRIEF DISAPPEARANCE OF TWO YEARS EARLIER.
THE SWARTHY COMPLEXION INDICATES A SEAMAN — AS DOES THE "SAILOR'S KNOT" AROUND THE VICTIM'S NECK.
SAILORS OFTEN RESIDE AT MME. ROGET'S PENSION, AND THE PERIOD BETWEEN THE TWO DISAPPEARANCES IS ABOUT THE DURATION OF A NAVAL VOYAGE.
THIS LOVER NO DOUBT RETURNED TO RESUME HIS ATTENTIONS UPON THE GIRL.
HE LURED HER TO THE WOODS — BUT SHE RESISTED HIM...
PROVOKING A FURIOUS ATTACK.
HE THEN ROWED THE BODY TO THE MIDDLE OF THE RIVER — THE DERELICT BOAT BEING FOUND THE NEXT DAY — AND MADE HIS ESCAPE.
(NO SUCH BOAT WAS EVER FOUND; A DETAIL FABRICATED BY THE AUTHOR.)
"THE MYSTERY OF MARIE ROGÊT" WAS AT LAST PURCHASED BY A RELATIVELY SEDATE PERIODICAL, SNOWDEN'S LADIES' COMPANION...
SNOWDEN'S LADIES' COMPANION
AND WAS PUBLISHED IN THREE PARTS — IN THEIR ISSUES OF NOVEMBER AND DECEMBER, 1842, AND FEBRUARY, 1843.

PART V.

THE MYSTERY OF MARY ROGERS.

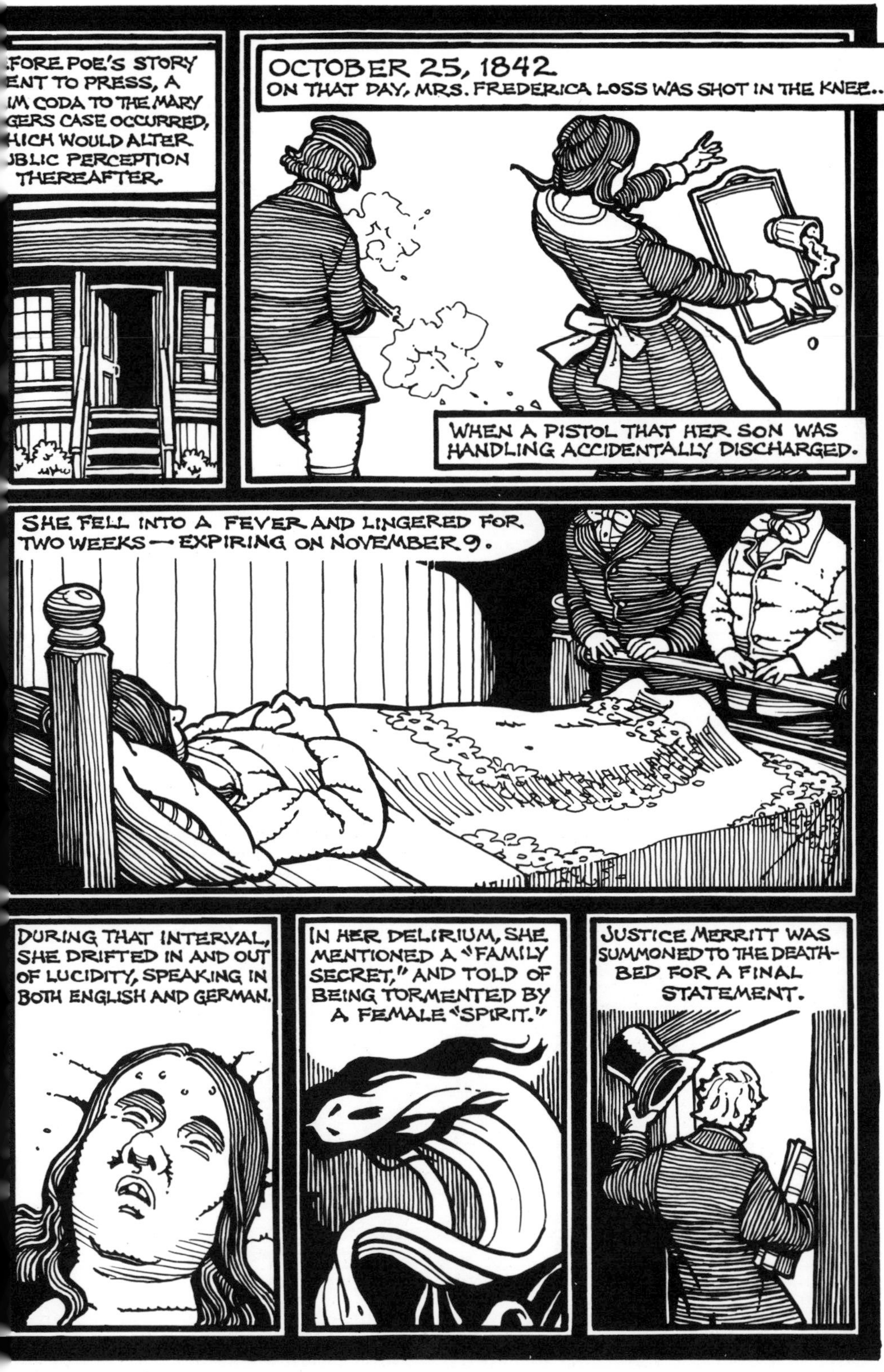

FORE POE'S STORY
ENT TO PRESS, A
IM CODA TO THE MARY
GERS CASE OCCURRED,
HICH WOULD ALTER
JBLIC PERCEPTION
THEREAFTER.
OCTOBER 25, 1842
ON THAT DAY, MRS. FREDERICA LOSS WAS SHOT IN THE KNEE...
WHEN A PISTOL THAT HER SON WAS HANDLING ACCIDENTALLY DISCHARGED.
SHE FELL INTO A FEVER AND LINGERED FOR TWO WEEKS — EXPIRING ON NOVEMBER 9.
DURING THAT INTERVAL, SHE DRIFTED IN AND OUT OF LUCIDITY, SPEAKING IN BOTH ENGLISH AND GERMAN.
IN HER DELIRIUM, SHE MENTIONED A "FAMILY SECRET," AND TOLD OF BEING TORMENTED BY A FEMALE "SPIRIT."
JUSTICE MERRITT WAS SUMMONED TO THE DEATH-BED FOR A FINAL STATEMENT.

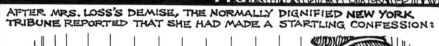

AFTER MRS. LOSS'S DEMISE, THE NORMALLY DIGNIFIED NEW YORK TRIBUNE REPORTED THAT SHE HAD MADE A STARTLING CONFESSION:

MARY ROGERS, SHE ADMITTED, HAD INDEED PERISHED UNDER HER ROOF—OF AN UNSUCCESSFUL ATTEMPT AT ABORTION.

THE UNNAMED PHYSICIAN, WHO HAD ACCOMPANIED MARY TO THE TAVERN, HELPED TO PLACE HER PARTIALLY-CLOTHED BODY IN THE RIVER.

THE REMAINING ARTICLES OF CLOTHING WERE SUNK INTO THE POND OF A NEARBY PROPERTY.

LATER, HOWEVER, THEY WERE REMOVED, FOR FEAR OF DISCOVERY, AND ARRANGED IN THE THICKET.

PUBLIC INTEREST IN THE CASE IGNITED ANEW...

AND THE WOODS, ONCE AGAIN, OVER-RUN WITH CURIOUS SIGHT-SEERS.

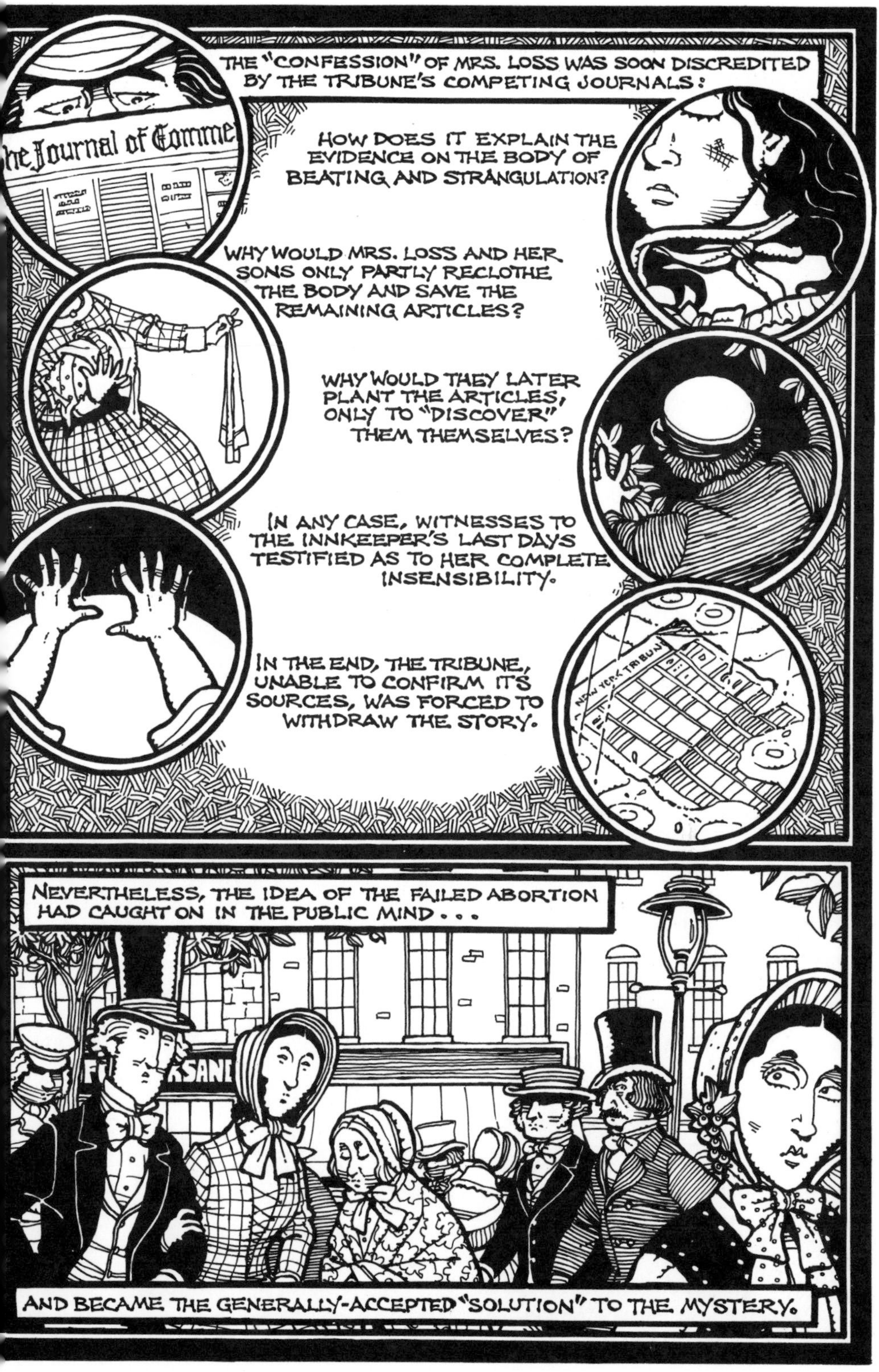
THE "CONFESSION" OF MRS. LOSS WAS SOON DISCREDITED BY THE TRIBUNE'S COMPETING JOURNALS:
The Journal of Comme
HOW DOES IT EXPLAIN THE EVIDENCE ON THE BODY OF BEATING AND STRANGULATION?
WHY WOULD MRS. LOSS AND HER SONS ONLY PARTLY RECLOTHE THE BODY AND SAVE THE REMAINING ARTICLES?
WHY WOULD THEY LATER PLANT THE ARTICLES, ONLY TO "DISCOVER" THEM THEMSELVES?
IN ANY CASE, WITNESSES TO THE INNKEEPER'S LAST DAYS TESTIFIED AS TO HER COMPLETE INSENSIBILITY.
IN THE END, THE TRIBUNE, UNABLE TO CONFIRM IT'S SOURCES, WAS FORCED TO WITHDRAW THE STORY.
NEW YORK TRIBUN
NEVERTHELESS, THE IDEA OF THE FAILED ABORTION HAD CAUGHT ON IN THE PUBLIC MIND . . .
AND BECAME THE GENERALLY-ACCEPTED "SOLUTION" TO THE MYSTERY.

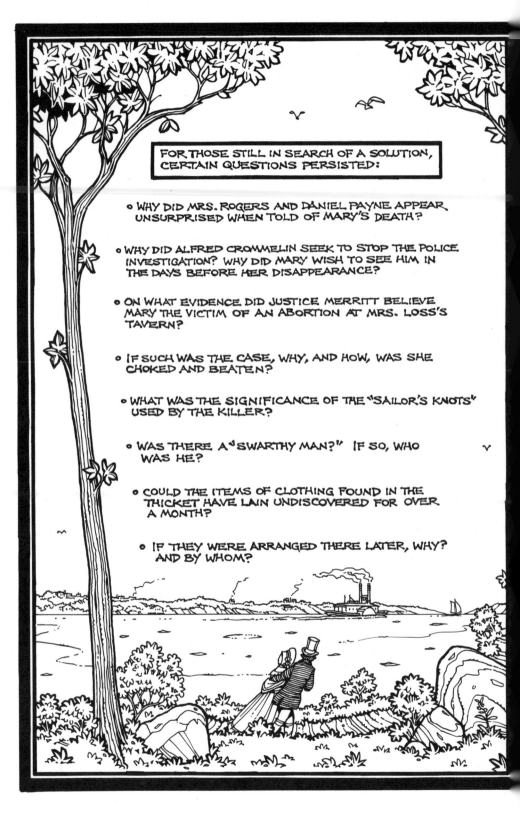

FOR THOSE STILL IN SEARCH OF A SOLUTION, CERTAIN QUESTIONS PERSISTED:

- WHY DID MRS. ROGERS AND DANIEL PAYNE APPEAR UNSURPRISED WHEN TOLD OF MARY'S DEATH?

- WHY DID ALFRED CROMMELIN SEEK TO STOP THE POLICE INVESTIGATION? WHY DID MARY WISH TO SEE HIM IN THE DAYS BEFORE HER DISAPPEARANCE?

- ON WHAT EVIDENCE DID JUSTICE MERRITT BELIEVE MARY THE VICTIM OF AN ABORTION AT MRS. LOSS'S TAVERN?

- IF SUCH WAS THE CASE, WHY, AND HOW, WAS SHE CHOKED AND BEATEN?

- WHAT WAS THE SIGNIFICANCE OF THE "SAILOR'S KNOTS" USED BY THE KILLER?

- WAS THERE A "SWARTHY MAN?" IF SO, WHO WAS HE?

- COULD THE ITEMS OF CLOTHING FOUND IN THE THICKET HAVE LAIN UNDISCOVERED FOR OVER A MONTH?

- IF THEY WERE ARRANGED THERE LATER, WHY? AND BY WHOM?

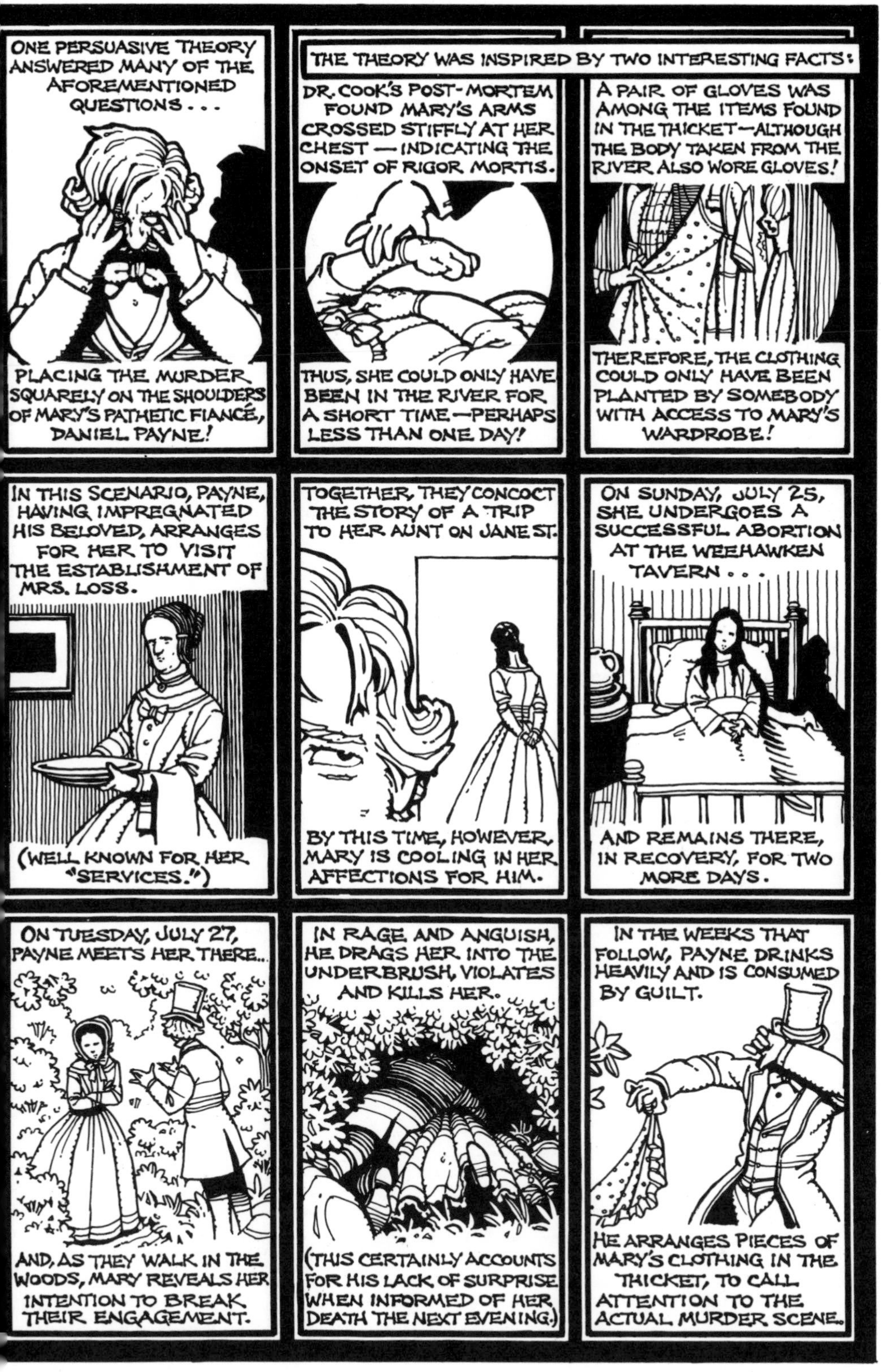
ONE PERSUASIVE THEORY ANSWERED MANY OF THE AFOREMENTIONED QUESTIONS . . .
PLACING THE MURDER SQUARELY ON THE SHOULDERS OF MARY'S PATHETIC FIANCÉ, DANIEL PAYNE!
THE THEORY WAS INSPIRED BY TWO INTERESTING FACTS:
DR. COOK'S POST-MORTEM FOUND MARY'S ARMS CROSSED STIFFLY AT HER CHEST — INDICATING THE ONSET OF RIGOR MORTIS.
THUS, SHE COULD ONLY HAVE BEEN IN THE RIVER FOR A SHORT TIME—PERHAPS LESS THAN ONE DAY!
A PAIR OF GLOVES WAS AMONG THE ITEMS FOUND IN THE THICKET—ALTHOUGH THE BODY TAKEN FROM THE RIVER ALSO WORE GLOVES!
THEREFORE, THE CLOTHING COULD ONLY HAVE BEEN PLANTED BY SOMEBODY WITH ACCESS TO MARY'S WARDROBE!
IN THIS SCENARIO, PAYNE, HAVING IMPREGNATED HIS BELOVED, ARRANGES FOR HER TO VISIT THE ESTABLISHMENT OF MRS. LOSS.
(WELL KNOWN FOR HER "SERVICES.")
TOGETHER, THEY CONCOCT THE STORY OF A TRIP TO HER AUNT ON JANE ST.
BY THIS TIME, HOWEVER, MARY IS COOLING IN HER AFFECTIONS FOR HIM.
ON SUNDAY, JULY 25, SHE UNDERGOES A SUCCESSFUL ABORTION AT THE WEEHAWKEN TAVERN . . .
AND REMAINS THERE, IN RECOVERY, FOR TWO MORE DAYS.
ON TUESDAY, JULY 27, PAYNE MEETS HER THERE...
AND, AS THEY WALK IN THE WOODS, MARY REVEALS HER INTENTION TO BREAK THEIR ENGAGEMENT.
IN RAGE AND ANGUISH, HE DRAGS HER INTO THE UNDERBRUSH, VIOLATES AND KILLS HER.
(THIS CERTAINLY ACCOUNTS FOR HIS LACK OF SURPRISE WHEN INFORMED OF HER DEATH THE NEXT EVENING.)
IN THE WEEKS THAT FOLLOW, PAYNE DRINKS HEAVILY AND IS CONSUMED BY GUILT.
HE ARRANGES PIECES OF MARY'S CLOTHING IN THE THICKET, TO CALL ATTENTION TO THE ACTUAL MURDER SCENE.

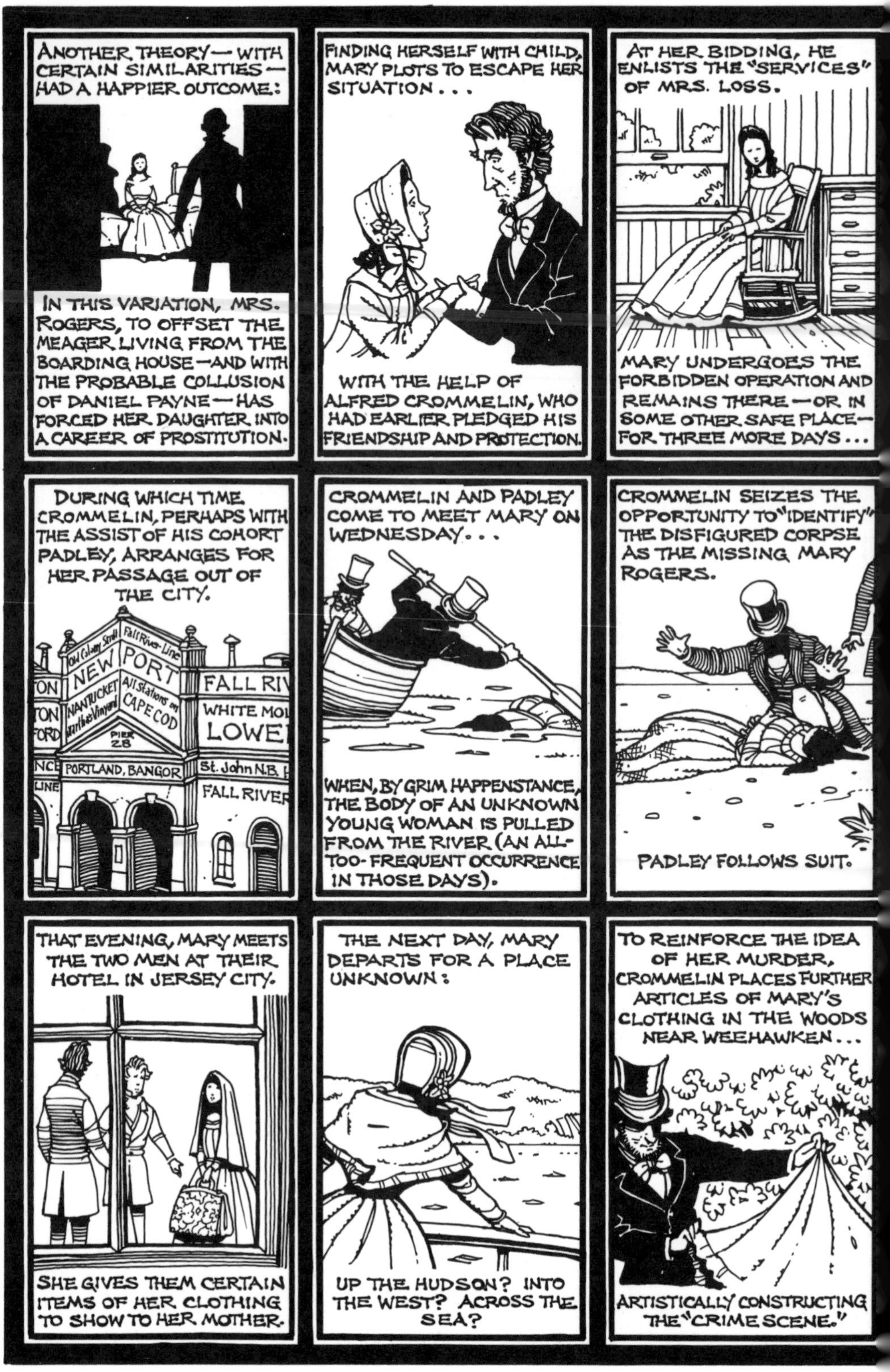
ANOTHER THEORY — WITH CERTAIN SIMILARITIES — HAD A HAPPIER OUTCOME:
IN THIS VARIATION, MRS. ROGERS, TO OFFSET THE MEAGER LIVING FROM THE BOARDING HOUSE — AND WITH THE PROBABLE COLLUSION OF DANIEL PAYNE — HAS FORCED HER DAUGHTER INTO A CAREER OF PROSTITUTION.
FINDING HERSELF WITH CHILD, MARY PLOTS TO ESCAPE HER SITUATION . . .
WITH THE HELP OF ALFRED CROMMELIN, WHO HAD EARLIER PLEDGED HIS FRIENDSHIP AND PROTECTION.
AT HER BIDDING, HE ENLISTS THE "SERVICES" OF MRS. LOSS.
MARY UNDERGOES THE FORBIDDEN OPERATION AND REMAINS THERE — OR IN SOME OTHER SAFE PLACE — FOR THREE MORE DAYS . . .
DURING WHICH TIME CROMMELIN, PERHAPS WITH THE ASSIST OF HIS COHORT PADLEY, ARRANGES FOR HER PASSAGE OUT OF THE CITY.
Old Colony Stroll
Fall River-Line
NEW PORT
NANTUCKET
Martha's Vineyard
All stations on CAPE COD
PIER 28
FALL RI
WHITE MO
LOWE
PORTLAND, BANGOR
St. John N.B.
FALL RIVER
CROMMELIN AND PADLEY COME TO MEET MARY ON WEDNESDAY . . .
WHEN, BY GRIM HAPPENSTANCE, THE BODY OF AN UNKNOWN YOUNG WOMAN IS PULLED FROM THE RIVER (AN ALL-TOO-FREQUENT OCCURRENCE IN THOSE DAYS).
CROMMELIN SEIZES THE OPPORTUNITY TO "IDENTIFY" THE DISFIGURED CORPSE AS THE MISSING MARY ROGERS.
PADLEY FOLLOWS SUIT.
THAT EVENING, MARY MEETS THE TWO MEN AT THEIR HOTEL IN JERSEY CITY.
SHE GIVES THEM CERTAIN ITEMS OF HER CLOTHING TO SHOW TO HER MOTHER.
THE NEXT DAY, MARY DEPARTS FOR A PLACE UNKNOWN:
UP THE HUDSON? INTO THE WEST? ACROSS THE SEA?
TO REINFORCE THE IDEA OF HER MURDER, CROMMELIN PLACES FURTHER ARTICLES OF MARY'S CLOTHING IN THE WOODS NEAR WEEHAWKEN . . .
ARTISTICALLY CONSTRUCTING THE "CRIME SCENE."

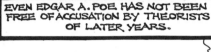

EVEN EDGAR A. POE HAS NOT BEEN FREE OF ACCUSATION BY THEORISTS OF LATER YEARS.

SHE COULD HAVE TAKEN PITY UPON HIS SORROWING SOUL AND ALLOWED HIM TO LURE HER TO A TRYST ON THE NEW JERSEY SHORE.

HE HAD BEEN, AFTER ALL, ACQUAINTED WITH MARY ROGERS, AND, THOUGH RESIDENT IN PHILADELPHIA, HAD AMPLE OPPORTUNITY TO VISIT NEW YORK.

WELL KNOWN WAS HIS WEAKNESS FOR ALCOHOL—WHICH WOULD DRIVE HIM OCCASIONALLY TO GIVE WAY TO A MAD IMPULSE.

AS THINGS ACTUALLY HAPPENED, POE MOVED HIS FAMILY TO NEW YORK CITY IN 1845...

WHERE HE AT LAST GAINED A MEASURE OF FAME WITH THE PUBLICATION OF HIS POEM "THE RAVEN,"

HIS COLLECTED TALES, ALSO PUBLISHED THAT YEAR, CONTAINED A REVISED VERSION OF "THE MYSTERY OF MARIE ROGÊT."

BY THAT TIME, THE "SOLUTION" OF THE FAILED ABORTION WAS FIRMLY ENTRENCHED IN THE PUBLIC MIND...

AND SO POE HAD CLEVERLY ALTERED A FEW SENTENCES TO ALLOW FOR THAT CONCLUSION.

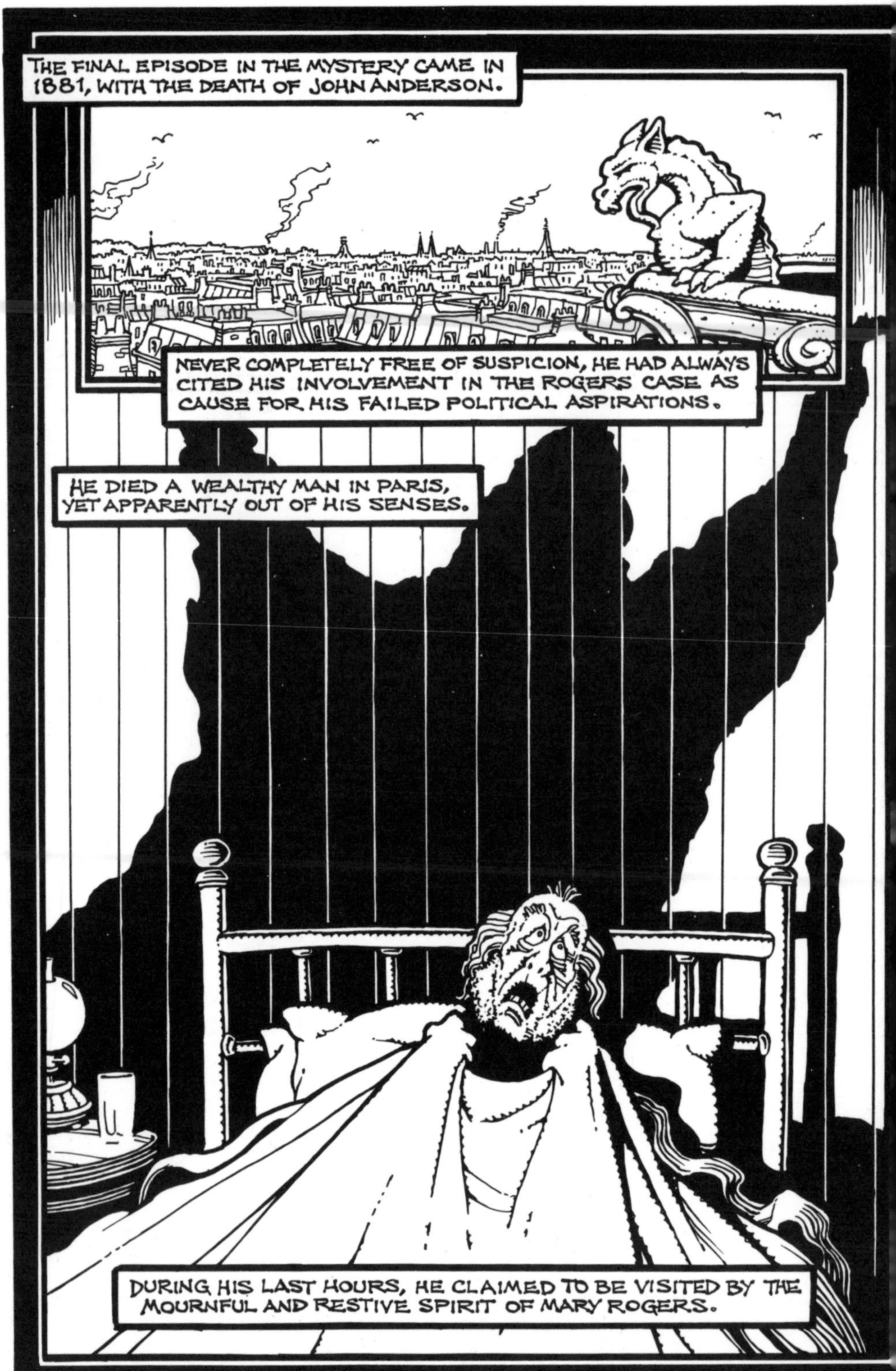
THE FINAL EPISODE IN THE MYSTERY CAME IN 1881, WITH THE DEATH OF JOHN ANDERSON.
NEVER COMPLETELY FREE OF SUSPICION, HE HAD ALWAYS CITED HIS INVOLVEMENT IN THE ROGERS CASE AS CAUSE FOR HIS FAILED POLITICAL ASPIRATIONS.
HE DIED A WEALTHY MAN IN PARIS, YET APPARENTLY OUT OF HIS SENSES.
DURING HIS LAST HOURS, HE CLAIMED TO BE VISITED BY THE MOURNFUL AND RESTIVE SPIRIT OF MARY ROGERS.

TODAY, NO HEAD-STONE OR MONUMENT MARKS THE MEMORY OF MARY CECILIA ROGERS.

HER FINAL RESTING-PLACE, IN FACT, REMAINS UNKNOWN.

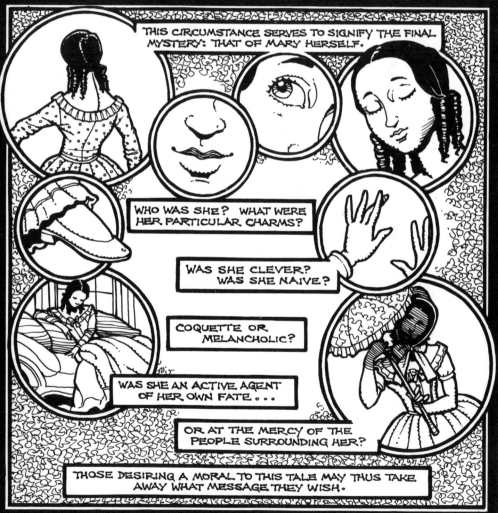

THIS CIRCUMSTANCE SERVES TO SIGNIFY THE FINAL MYSTERY: THAT OF MARY HERSELF.

WHO WAS SHE? WHAT WERE HER PARTICULAR CHARMS?

WAS SHE CLEVER? WAS SHE NAIVE?

COQUETTE OR MELANCHOLIC?

WAS SHE AN ACTIVE AGENT OF HER OWN FATE...

OR AT THE MERCY OF THE PEOPLE SURROUNDING HER?

THOSE DESIRING A MORAL TO THIS TALE MAY THUS TAKE AWAY WHAT MESSAGE THEY WISH.

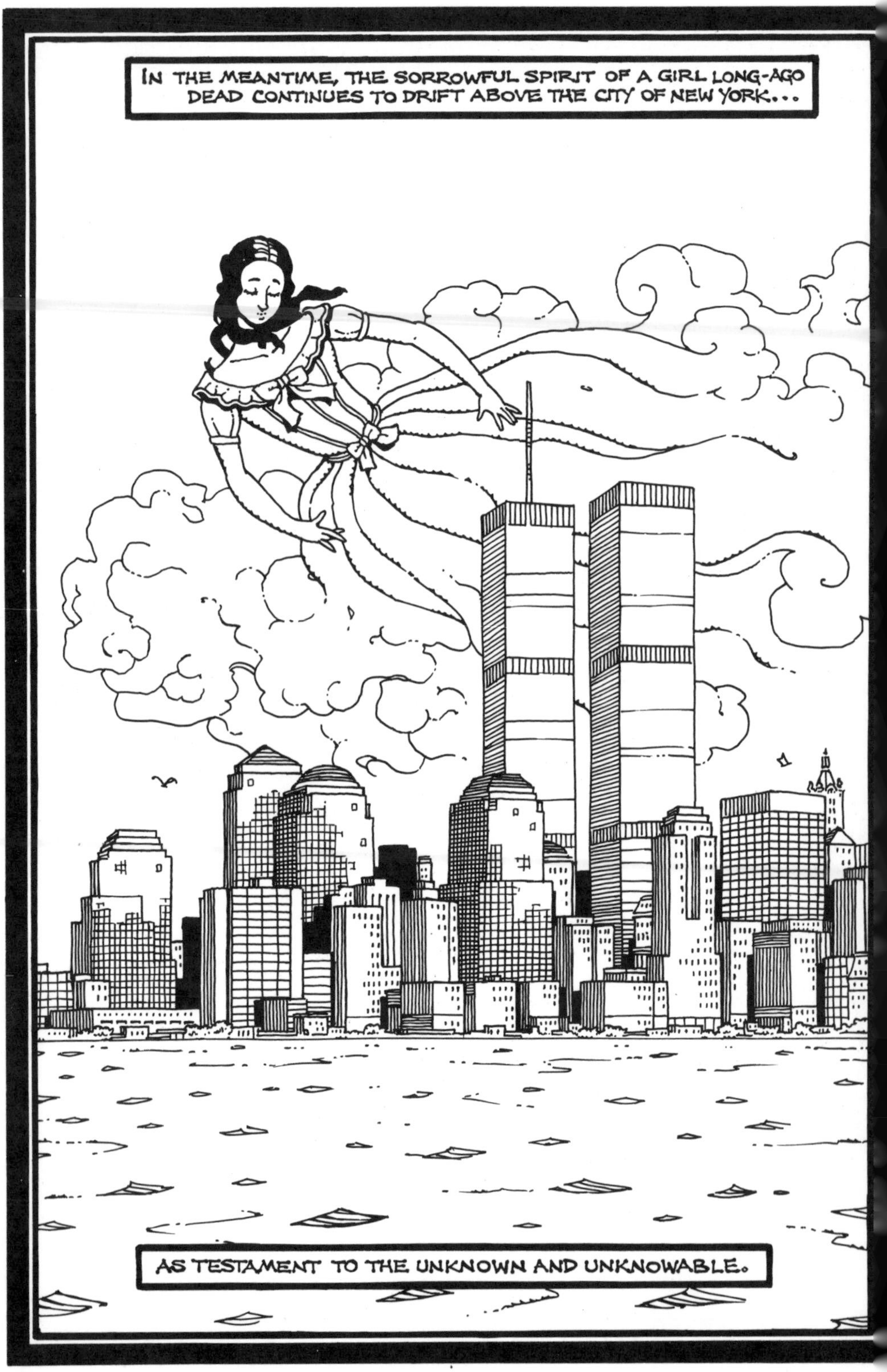
IN THE MEANTIME, THE SORROWFUL SPIRIT OF A GIRL LONG-AGO DEAD CONTINUES TO DRIFT ABOVE THE CITY OF NEW YORK...
AS TESTAMENT TO THE UNKNOWN AND UNKNOWABLE.